Management Information systems - MIS

Business strategy books, Volume 4

SANJIVAN SAINI

Published by SANJIVAN SAINI, 2023.

MANAGEMENT INFORMATION SYSTEMS - MIS

First edition. November 2, 2023.

ISBN: 979-8223302810

Written by SANJIVAN SAINI.

Also by SANJIVAN SAINI

Business strategy books

Procedure and Documentation in Supply Chain Management
Exploring the Fundamentals of Database Management Systems
Cold chain Business Planning and Strategy: Design, Retrofit And Maintenance Of Cold Storages And Pack Houses
Management Information systems - MIS

Standalone

Logistics in Manufacturing, Supply Chain, and Distribution
E-commerce
Engineering Economics & Accountancy :Managerial Economics
The Essence of Innovation
Introduction to Reverse Logistics
Material Handling Repair and Maintenance of Equipment
Port Terminals System - Conveyor and Equipment Maintenance
"Packaging
����� ��������-3: ����� �� ���
����� ���
����, ������ �� ���� ������
Fundamentals of Logistics and Warehousing

Table of Contents

BOOK OVERVIEW

"Management Information System" by Sanjivan Saini is a comprehensive book that covers various aspects of Management Information Systems (MIS) and Enterprise Resource Planning (ERP). It provides readers with a deep understanding of the key concepts, principles, and applications related to MIS and ERP. The book is structured into different units, each focusing on essential topics in the field of MIS and ERP. Here is an overview of the units included in the book:

Unit 1: MIS - Introduction

This unit serves as an introduction to Management Information Systems (MIS). It covers the fundamental concepts, objectives, and benefits of MIS in modern organizations. Readers gain insights into the role of MIS in decision-making, planning, and overall business management.

Unit 2: Planning

In this unit, the book delves into the significance of planning in the context of MIS. It explores how MIS aids in strategic planning, operational planning, and resource allocation. The unit may cover topics such as forecasting, budgeting, and performance planning.

Unit 3: Decision Making

This unit focuses on decision-making processes and how MIS supports informed decision-making. It explores various decision-making models, techniques, and tools enabled by MIS. Topics may include data analysis, business intelligence, and reporting.

Unit 4: ERP - Introduction

This unit provides an introduction to Enterprise Resource Planning (ERP) systems. It covers the basics of ERP, its benefits, and its role in integrating business processes. Topics may include ERP modules, implementation considerations, and ERP lifecycle.

Unit 5: ERP Dynamics

Building upon the previous unit, this section delves deeper into ERP dynamics, including system design, customization, and integration. It may explore the different ERP software available in the market and their functionalities.

Unit 6: Managerial Decision Making

In this unit, the book may focus specifically on managerial decision-making processes within the context of MIS and ERP. It may cover decision support systems, data analytics, and predictive modeling.

Unit 7: Data Management

This unit provides insights into the management of data within MIS and ERP systems. It covers data storage, data security, data integrity, and data governance.

Unit 8: File Design and Program Design

This unit delves into file design and program design principles in the context of MIS and ERP systems. It may cover database design, file organization, and programming languages used in ERP systems.

The book appears to provide a comprehensive understanding of Management Information Systems, their role in decision-making and planning, and the importance and dynamics of Enterprise Resource Planning systems. It may be useful for students, professionals, and anyone interested in learning about the concepts, principles, and applications of MIS and ERP in modern business environments.

As the book's contents are outlined in this overview, readers can expect to gain insights into the topics mentioned above and understand how MIS and ERP contribute to organizational efficiency, effectiveness, and decision-making processes.

UNIT-1 MIS - INTRODUCTION

LESSON OUTLINE-

- ❖ MIS - INTRODUCTION
- ❖ The meaning and use MIS, System View of Business,
- ❖ Process of MIS, Development of MIS within the organization,
- ❖ Management Process,
- ❖ Information Needs,
- ❖ System Approach in Planning Organizing and
- ❖ Controlling MIS

1.1 MIS - INTRODUCTION

MIS stands for "Management Information System." It is a comprehensive system that provides managers and decision-makers at all levels of an organization with the information they need to make informed decisions effectively. MIS plays a crucial role in collecting, processing, storing, and disseminating data in a structured manner to support the decision-making process.

The main purpose of an MIS is to transform raw data into meaningful and actionable information, enabling managers to monitor the organization's performance, identify trends and patterns, and make strategic decisions to achieve the organization's objectives. It serves as a bridge between technology, data, and business processes.

Key components of a Management Information System typically include:

1. **Data Input**: The system collects data from various sources, such as internal databases, external sources, and user inputs.
2. **Data Processing:** The collected data undergoes processing, which involves organizing, analyzing, and summarizing it to generate useful information.
3. **Data Storage:** The processed information is stored in databases or data warehouses for easy retrieval and future reference.
4. **Information Output:** The MIS generates reports, charts, graphs, and other visual representations to present the information to decision-makers.
5. **Decision Support:** MIS provides tools and models for decision support, helping managers analyze scenarios and make well-informed choices.
6. **Communication**: MIS facilitates the sharing and communication of information among different departments and levels within the organization.

MIS can be tailored to different organizational needs, including financial MIS, marketing MIS, human resources MIS, and more. Implementing an effective MIS can lead to several benefits, such as improved decision-making, enhanced efficiency, better resource allocation, and competitive advantage in the market.

It's worth noting that with advancements in technology, modern MIS systems often incorporate elements of artificial intelligence, big data analytics, and business intelligence tools to handle larger and more complex datasets, thereby enabling organizations to gain deeper insights and stay ahead in a rapidly evolving business environment.

1.2 Meaning of MIS:

Management Information System (MIS) is a computer-based system that collects, processes, stores, and disseminates information to support decision-making, coordination, control, analysis, and visualization of an organization's operations. It helps managers at different levels of an organization to access relevant data and turn it into valuable information for effective planning and strategic decision-making.

Uses of MIS:

1. **Decision-making support**: MIS provides timely and accurate information to managers, enabling them to make informed decisions based on data analysis and insights. It assists in both routine operational decisions and strategic long-term planning.
2. **Planning and forecasting**: With historical and real-time data available, MIS aids in forecasting future trends and outcomes. Managers can create business plans and set achievable goals using this information.
3. **Resource management:** MIS facilitates the efficient allocation of resources, including human resources, finances, and materials, optimizing their utilization and reducing wastage.
4. **Performance monitoring:** It helps monitor the organization's performance by generating various reports and key performance indicators (KPIs). Managers can assess progress and identify areas for improvement.
5. **Business process optimization**: MIS identifies bottlenecks and inefficiencies in business processes, allowing organizations to streamline their operations for improved productivity.
6. **Strategic advantage:** Having access to relevant and up-to-

date information enables organizations to respond quickly to market changes, giving them a competitive edge over others.

7. **Communication and collaboration**: MIS promotes seamless communication and collaboration between different departments and levels within the organization, fostering a more cohesive and efficient work environment.
8. **Data security and integrity:** MIS includes measures to safeguard data, ensuring that sensitive information remains protected from unauthorized access and manipulation.
9. **Business intelligence**: Modern MIS often integrates business intelligence tools, data analytics, and reporting capabilities, providing deeper insights and data visualizations for better understanding and decision-making.
10. **Compliance and reporting**: MIS can help organizations meet regulatory requirements by generating reports that adhere to specific standards and guidelines.

IN SUMMARY, MANAGEMENT Information System (MIS) plays a crucial role in supporting managerial decision-making, optimizing business processes, and enhancing overall organizational efficiency. It is an essential tool for businesses to succeed and adapt in an increasingly data-driven and competitive landscape.

1.3 System View of Business

The system view of business refers to the perspective that views an organization as a complex and interconnected system rather than a collection of isolated and independent parts. This view considers the various components and functions within a business as interrelated and interdependent, operating together to achieve common goals and objectives.

In the system view, a business is seen as a dynamic entity that interacts with its internal and external environment. Changes in one part of the system can have ripple effects on other parts, influencing the overall performance of the organization. It emphasizes that the success and effectiveness of a business rely on the effective coordination and integration of its various components.

Key aspects of the system view of business include:

1. **Holistic Perspective:** The system view takes a holistic approach, considering the entire organization as a unified and interconnected entity. It recognizes that actions taken in one area of the business can impact other areas, and decisions must be made with the overall system in mind.
2. **Inputs, Processes, and Outputs**: The system view analyzes the inputs (resources and information) that go into the organization, the processes (activities and operations) that transform these inputs, and the outputs (products, services, and outcomes) that result from these processes.
3. **Interdependence**: Different departments, functions, and teams within a business are interconnected and rely on each other to achieve common goals. Collaboration and effective communication are essential to ensure smooth operations.
4. **Feedback Loops**: The system view incorporates feedback loops, which means that information on the outcomes of certain actions or decisions is used to adjust and improve future actions.
5. **Open System**: Businesses are considered open systems that interact with their external environment, including customers, suppliers, competitors, regulatory bodies, and the broader market. The external environment can influence the organization, and the organization, in turn, can impact its environment.
6. **Complexity and Emergence**: Complex interactions and relationships between different elements within the business can lead to emergent properties or behaviors that may not

be evident when **examining individual components in isolation.**

7. **Adaptation and Change**: The system view acknowledges that businesses must be adaptable to changes in their environment. It encourages continuous improvement and learning to respond effectively to internal and external changes.

Applying the system view of business helps managers and decision-makers understand the organization in a more comprehensive and interconnected manner. It promotes a more strategic and holistic approach to problem-solving, encouraging a focus on optimizing the entire system rather than isolated parts. By understanding how the components of the business interact and affect each other, organizations can better align their efforts and resources to achieve their objectives efficiently.

1.4 Process of MIS

The process of Management Information System (MIS) involves several interconnected steps to ensure the effective collection, processing, storage, and dissemination of information within an organization. Below is an overview of the typical process of MIS:

1. **Data Collection**: The process begins with data collection from various sources, such as internal databases, external systems, sensors, surveys, or manual inputs. Data can be both structured (e.g., databases, spreadsheets) and unstructured (e.g., emails, documents).
2. **Data Processing**: Once the data is collected, it needs to be processed and transformed into meaningful information. Data processing involves activities like data cleaning (to remove errors and inconsistencies), data integration (to combine data from different sources), and data

transformation (to convert data into a usable format).

3. **Data Storage**: The processed information is then stored in databases or data warehouses. Data warehouses are specialized databases that allow for easy retrieval and analysis of large volumes of historical and current data.
4. **Information Analysis**: MIS performs data analysis to extract valuable insights, trends, patterns, and key performance indicators (KPIs) from the stored information. This step involves using various tools and techniques, such as data mining, business intelligence, and statistical analysis.
5. **Information Presentation**: The analyzed information is presented in a comprehensible and visually appealing format. Reports, charts, graphs, dashboards, and other visualizations are generated to convey the information to decision-makers effectively.
6. **Decision Support**: MIS provides decision support by offering managers and decision-makers the necessary information and tools to make informed choices. This may involve creating interactive reports, "what-if" analysis, and scenario modeling.
7. **Information Dissemination**: The relevant information is distributed to the appropriate stakeholders, such as managers, executives, and operational teams, based on their roles and access rights. This can be done through email, shared drives, collaboration platforms, or specialized MIS portals.
8. **Feedback and Monitoring**: MIS incorporates feedback mechanisms to assess the impact of decisions made based on the provided information. Monitoring the outcomes helps in continuous improvement and adjustment of strategies.
9. **Security and Privacy**: An essential aspect of the MIS process is ensuring data security and privacy. This involves implementing measures to protect sensitive information from unauthorized access, ensuring compliance with data

protection regulations.

10. **System Maintenance and Upgrades**: MIS requires continuous maintenance and periodic upgrades to keep the system running smoothly, accommodate changing business needs, and address potential issues or vulnerabilities.
11. **Continuous Improvement**: The MIS process is not static. It should be continuously evaluated and improved to align with changing business requirements, technological advancements, and organizational goals.

The effectiveness of the MIS process depends on the quality of data, the accuracy of analysis, the relevance of information, and the usability of the outputs. A well-implemented MIS can significantly enhance an organization's decision-making capabilities and overall performance.

1.5 Development of MIS within the organization

The development of a Management Information System (MIS) within an organization is a structured and iterative process that involves several key stages. The successful development and implementation of an MIS require collaboration among different stakeholders, including top management, IT professionals, functional departments, and end-users. Below are the typical stages involved in the development of MIS within an organization:

1. **Identifying Information Needs:** The first step is to identify the information needs of the organization. This involves understanding the specific requirements of various departments and levels of management. Key stakeholders should be involved in the process to ensure that the MIS aligns with the organization's strategic goals and objectives.

2. **Defining Objectives and Scope:** Based on the identified information needs, clear objectives for the MIS project are established. The scope of the system is defined, outlining what functionalities it will cover and what data will be included.
3. **Gathering Requirements:** Detailed requirements are gathered from different stakeholders. This step involves conducting interviews, workshops, and surveys to understand the specific data elements, reports, and functionalities needed by each department.
4. **Designing the System:** The design phase involves creating a blueprint of the MIS. It includes designing the database structure, user interfaces, data flows, and the overall architecture of the system. User experience (UX) and usability considerations are also taken into account during this stage.
5. **Development and Testing:** With the design in place, the MIS is developed by a team of IT professionals and developers. This stage involves coding, creating the database, building interfaces, and integrating various components. Rigorous testing is conducted to identify and fix any bugs or issues.
6. **Data Integration:** Integrating data from different sources is a crucial aspect of MIS development. Data from various departments and systems need to be consolidated and standardized to ensure consistency and accuracy.
7. **Training and User Adoption:** Before the system is rolled out organization-wide, end-users need to be trained on how to use the MIS effectively. User adoption is essential for the success of the MIS, so proper training and change management efforts are vital.
8. **Deployment:** The MIS is deployed throughout the organization, and users start using it for their day-to-day

operations. A phased implementation approach may be adopted to minimize disruptions.

9. **Monitoring and Evaluation:** After the MIS is live, it is continuously monitored to ensure that it meets the organization's objectives and is performing as expected. Feedback from users is gathered to identify areas for improvement.
10. **Maintenance and Upgrades:** The MIS requires ongoing maintenance to keep it running smoothly. Regular updates and enhancements may be made to add new features, improve performance, and address issues.
11. **Continuous Improvement:** MIS development is an ongoing process. As the organization evolves and its needs change, the MIS must be adapted and improved to remain relevant and effective.

Throughout the development process, communication and collaboration between the IT team, management, and end-users are crucial. Additionally, cybersecurity measures should be implemented to safeguard sensitive information within the MIS. By following a structured development approach and involving all relevant stakeholders, an organization can build a robust MIS that enhances decision-making and supports its overall growth and success.

1.6 Management Process

The management process refers to the systematic approach used by managers to plan, organize, lead, and control the resources and activities within an organization to achieve its goals effectively and efficiently. It involves a series of interconnected steps that help managers make informed decisions and ensure that the organization's objectives are met. The management process typically includes the following key stages:

1. **Planning:** Planning is the foundation of the management process. It involves setting objectives, defining strategies, and outlining the course of action to achieve the organization's goals. During this stage, managers identify tasks, allocate resources, set timelines, and develop contingency plans to address potential challenges.
2. **Organizing:** Once the plans are in place, managers move to the organizing stage. This involves structuring the organization by defining roles, responsibilities, and reporting relationships. It also includes creating departments, teams, and workgroups to ensure that the necessary tasks are carried out efficiently.
3. **Leading:** Leadership is about inspiring, guiding, and motivating employees to work towards the organization's goals. Effective leaders communicate the vision, set clear expectations, and provide support to their teams. They encourage collaboration, foster a positive work environment, and address any issues that arise during the execution of plans.
4. **Controlling:** Controlling is the process of monitoring performance and comparing it to the established goals. It involves measuring actual results, identifying deviations from the plans, and taking corrective actions as needed. This stage ensures that the organization stays on track and makes necessary adjustments to achieve its objectives.

These stages are not always sequential and can overlap, especially in dynamic and complex environments. Managers continually cycle through these processes to respond to changes in the internal and external business environment.

Key characteristics of the management process include:

- **Decision-Making:** Managers must make decisions at each stage of the process, based on available information and analysis. Effective decision-making is critical for achieving desired outcomes.

- **Communication:** Successful management requires effective communication at all levels of the organization. Clear and open communication ensures that everyone understands the goals, plans, and their roles in achieving them.
- **Flexibility:** The management process should be flexible enough to adapt to changes and uncertainties in the business environment. This adaptability allows managers to respond quickly to challenges and opportunities.
- **Continuous Improvement:** Managers should seek ways to improve the management process continuously. Learning from experiences, feedback, and best practices helps optimize future decision-making and performance.
- **Ethics and Social Responsibility:** Responsible and ethical management considers the impact of decisions and actions on stakeholders, including employees, customers, society, and the environment.
- **Alignment with Strategy:** The management process should align with the organization's overall strategy. Each decision and action should contribute to the achievement of long-term goals.

Effective management ensures that resources are utilized efficiently, risks are mitigated, and the organization remains competitive and sustainable in a rapidly changing world. It is a dynamic and ongoing process that requires adaptability, leadership, and a commitment to achieving the organization's objectives.

1.7 Information Needs

Information needs refer to the specific requirements for data, facts, and insights that individuals or organizations seek to support their decision-making, problem-solving, and overall operational effectiveness. These needs vary depending on the context, roles, and goals of the individuals or entities involved. Understanding information needs is crucial in designing effective systems, such as Management Information Systems (MIS) or Business Intelligence (BI) solutions, to provide relevant and timely information to stakeholders.

Information needs can be classified into various categories:

1. **Operational Information Needs:** These are the day-to-day information requirements necessary for the routine functioning of an organization. They include data related to sales transactions, inventory levels, production schedules, customer inquiries, and other operational processes.
2. **Tactical Information Needs:** Tactical information needs are associated with mid-level managers and are focused on implementing the strategies defined by higher management. These needs include data about departmental performance, resource allocation, workforce productivity, and budget monitoring.
3. **Strategic Information Needs:** Strategic information needs pertain to top-level executives and involve information critical for long-term planning and decision-making. This includes industry trends, market analysis, competitive intelligence, and potential growth opportunities.
4. **External Information Needs:** These refer to the information required from external sources, such as market research reports, economic indicators, industry publications, or data from regulatory bodies. External information helps organizations understand market conditions and external

influences on their business.

5. **Internal Information Needs:** Internal information needs encompass data generated from within the organization. This may include financial reports, sales figures, employee performance data, and customer feedback collected through internal surveys.
6. **Real-time Information Needs:** Certain situations and industries demand real-time or near-real-time information. For example, financial trading companies require up-to-the-second data on stock prices and market fluctuations to make rapid investment decisions.
7. **Predictive Information Needs:** Predictive information needs involve data and insights used to forecast future trends, customer behavior, demand patterns, and potential risks. Predictive analytics and forecasting techniques are applied to address these needs.
8. **Compliance and Regulatory Information Needs:** Organizations may require specific information to ensure compliance with laws, regulations, and industry standards. This includes financial reporting, environmental impact data, and employee safety records.

Identifying and understanding information needs are critical steps in the development of information systems and decision support tools. Organizations need to gather and analyze these needs from various stakeholders, including managers, executives, employees, customers, and external partners, to tailor information solutions that align with the organization's objectives and support informed decision-making across all levels. By addressing information needs effectively, organizations can gain a competitive advantage, enhance efficiency, and improve overall performance.

1.8 System Approach in Planning

Organizing and Controlling MIS.

The system approach in planning, organizing, and controlling Management Information System (MIS) involves applying a holistic and integrated perspective to ensure the effective development, implementation, and management of the MIS within an organization. The system approach emphasizes the interdependence and interconnectedness of the different components and processes involved in MIS, as well as their alignment with the overall goals of the organization. Here's how the system approach is applied in each of the stages:

Planning with a System Approach:

- **Identify Information Needs**: Understand the information needs of various stakeholders and departments within the organization. This involves considering both the specific requirements of each unit and how they relate to the overall organizational objectives.
- **Define Objectives**: Set clear objectives for the MIS, ensuring they align with the strategic goals of the organization. Determine the scope and functionality required to meet the information needs effectively.
- **Consider Interdependencies**: Recognize that different functional areas within the organization are interrelated and rely on each other for data and information. Plan for data integration and information sharing between departments to avoid silos.
- **Assess Resource Requirements**: Identify the resources (financial, human, and technological) necessary for developing and maintaining the MIS. Take into account the

potential impacts on existing systems and processes.

Organizing with a System Approach:

- **Establish Cross-Functional Teams**: Form cross-functional teams involving representatives from different departments to ensure a comprehensive understanding of information needs and requirements.
- **Create a Centralized Data Repository**: Develop a centralized database or data warehouse to store and manage the organization's data. This promotes data consistency, reduces redundancy, and facilitates easy data access for multiple users.
- **Integrate Data Sources**: Integrate data from various sources across the organization to provide a unified and coherent view of information to all stakeholders.
- **Define User Roles and Access Rights**: Establish user roles and access levels based on job responsibilities and security requirements, ensuring data confidentiality and integrity.

Controlling with a System Approach:

- **Monitor Key Performance Indicators (KPIs):** Define and track KPIs related to the performance of the MIS and its impact on organizational objectives. Use the KPIs to assess the effectiveness of the MIS and identify areas for improvement.
- **Implement Feedback Mechanisms**: Establish feedback loops to gather input from end-users and managers regarding the usability and functionality of the MIS. Use this feedback to make necessary adjustments and updates.
- **Continuously Improve the MIS**: Apply a continuous

improvement approach to the MIS by identifying bottlenecks, addressing inefficiencies, and upgrading the system to keep pace with technological advancements and changing business needs.

- **Ensure Alignment with Organizational Goals**: Regularly assess the MIS's alignment with the organization's strategic objectives. Make adjustments to the MIS to ensure it continues to support the organization's changing needs and priorities.

BY APPLYING THE SYSTEM approach in planning, organizing, and controlling the MIS, organizations can develop a comprehensive and efficient information system that meets the needs of all stakeholders, fosters collaboration, and contributes to the overall success and competitiveness of the organization.

UNIT-2. PLANNING

LESSON OUTLINE-

- Planning,
- Implementation and Controlling of Management Information System.
- Fundamentals of Data Processing,
- Computer Operation of Manual Information System,
- Components of Computer Systems,
- Flow Chart, and Conversion of Manual to Computer Based Systems,
- Computer Systems Software, Application Software, and Telecommunication Modem.

2.1 Planning

Planning is a fundamental management function that involves the process of setting objectives, determining the course of action, and developing strategies to achieve specific goals or desired outcomes. It is a forward-looking process that provides a roadmap for the organization's future actions and decisions. Planning is a crucial activity that lays the foundation for effective decision-making and ensures that resources are allocated in the most efficient and productive manner. Here are the key aspects and steps involved in the planning process:

1. **Establishing Objectives:** The planning process begins with defining clear and specific objectives. Objectives are the desired outcomes or results that the organization aims to achieve within a certain timeframe. These objectives should be SMART (Specific, Measurable, Achievable, Relevant, and Time-bound) to provide a clear direction for the organization.
2. **Environmental Analysis:** Before developing a plan, managers must analyze the internal and external environment that the organization operates in. This involves assessing strengths, weaknesses, opportunities, and threats (SWOT analysis) to identify factors that may impact the organization's ability to achieve its objectives.
3. **Formulating Strategies:** Based on the environmental analysis and established objectives, managers develop strategies to guide the organization towards its goals. Strategies are broad plans of action that outline how the organization will utilize its resources and capabilities to gain a competitive advantage or overcome challenges.
4. **Developing Action Plans:** Once strategies are in place, action plans are created to detail the specific steps, tasks, and timelines required to implement the strategies effectively. Action plans break down the overall strategy into actionable tasks that are assigned to responsible individuals or teams.
5. **Resource Allocation:** Planning involves allocating resources such as finances, personnel, technology, and materials to support the implementation of the action plans. Resource allocation ensures that the organization has the necessary means to carry out the planned activities.

6. **Flexibility and Contingency Planning:** Planning should incorporate flexibility to accommodate changes and uncertainties in the business environment. Contingency plans are developed to address potential risks and unexpected events that may affect the execution of the primary plan.
7. **Communication and Collaboration:** Effective planning requires clear communication of objectives, strategies, and action plans to all relevant stakeholders within the organization. Collaboration and involvement of key team members foster ownership and commitment to the plan's success.
8. **Monitoring and Review:** The planning process doesn't end with implementation. Regular monitoring and review of progress against the established objectives and milestones are crucial. This allows managers to assess the plan's effectiveness, identify deviations, and make necessary adjustments to keep the organization on track.
9. **Continuous Improvement:** Planning is an iterative process. Organizations must continuously learn from their experiences, measure outcomes, and use feedback to refine future planning efforts.

Effective planning is essential for organizations to achieve their goals, respond to changing circumstances, and remain competitive in a dynamic business environment. It provides a sense of direction and purpose, helping to align efforts across the organization and ensuring that everyone is working towards common objectives.

2.2 Implementation and Controlling of Management Information System

Implementation and controlling of a Management Information System (MIS) are critical stages in the process of successfully integrating the system into an organization and ensuring its effective and efficient operation. Let's look at each of these stages in detail:

1. Implementation of MIS:

- **Project Planning:** Develop a comprehensive project plan that outlines the scope, objectives, timeline, resource requirements, and responsibilities for implementing the MIS. This plan should consider the organization's specific needs and constraints.
- **System Development:** Depending on the chosen MIS solution (custom-built or off-the-shelf), the development team designs, configures, and customizes the system according to the organization's requirements. This includes database design, user interface development, and integration with existing systems.
- **Testing and Quality Assurance:** Rigorous testing is conducted to ensure that the MIS functions correctly, delivers accurate results, and meets user requirements. Quality assurance processes identify and resolve any defects or issues before deployment.
- **User Training:** Users and stakeholders must be trained on how to use the MIS effectively. Training sessions should cover system functionalities, data input procedures, report generation, and accessing relevant information.
- **Data Migration and Integration:** Existing data from different sources may need to be migrated and integrated into the new MIS. This ensures historical data is accessible and provides continuity for decision-making.
- **Pilot Implementation:** Deploy the MIS on a smaller scale in specific departments or regions to validate its functionality

and gather feedback from users. This pilot phase helps identify potential challenges and allows for adjustments before full-scale implementation.

- **Full-Scale Rollout:** Based on the lessons learned from the pilot phase, deploy the MIS organization-wide. Communication and change management strategies are essential to ensure a smooth transition and user adoption.

2. Controlling of MIS:

- **Monitoring Key Performance Indicators (KPIs):** Identify and track KPIs that measure the performance and effectiveness of the MIS. These KPIs can include system uptime, data accuracy, response times, user satisfaction, and adherence to service-level agreements.
- **Data Quality Control:** Regularly audit and validate the data entered into the MIS to ensure accuracy, completeness, and consistency. Implement data validation rules and error-checking mechanisms to maintain data integrity.
- **Security and Access Control:** Implement robust security measures to protect the MIS from unauthorized access, data breaches, and cyber threats. Assign access rights and user permissions based on roles and responsibilities.
- **Feedback and Continuous Improvement:** Gather feedback from end-users and stakeholders on their experience with the MIS. Use this feedback to identify areas for improvement, address user concerns, and optimize system performance.
- **Issue Resolution and Support:** Establish a support system to address user issues, system glitches, and technical problems promptly. Maintain a helpdesk or support team to provide assistance when needed.

- **Regular System Maintenance:** Perform routine maintenance tasks, such as updates, patches, and system backups, to keep the MIS running smoothly and securely. Address technical issues promptly to avoid disruptions.
- **Data Analytics and Insights:** Utilize data analytics tools and techniques to gain valuable insights from the data collected by the MIS. These insights can support better decision-making and strategic planning.
- **Compliance and Governance:** Ensure that the MIS adheres to relevant industry standards, data protection regulations, and organizational policies. Implement governance measures to oversee MIS operations and ensure compliance.

BY EFFECTIVELY IMPLEMENTING and controlling the MIS, organizations can optimize their decision-making processes, improve operational efficiency, and gain a competitive advantage through better access to accurate and timely information. Continuous monitoring, feedback, and improvement are essential to keep the MIS aligned with changing business needs and technological advancements.

2.3 Fundamentals of Data Processing

Fundamentals of data processing refer to the foundational principles and key concepts involved in the handling, manipulation, and transformation of data to produce meaningful and valuable information. Data processing is an essential component of various information systems and plays a crucial role in generating insights and supporting decision-making. Here are the key fundamentals of data processing:

1. **Data Collection:** Data processing begins with the collection of raw data from various sources, such as sensors, databases, surveys, forms, or user inputs. The quality and accuracy of

data collection directly impact the reliability of the processed information.

2. **Data Entry:** Data must be entered into the system in a structured and consistent manner. This involves organizing and recording data into fields, records, and files for further processing.
3. **Data Validation:** Data validation is the process of verifying the accuracy, integrity, and reliability of the collected data. It ensures that the data conforms to predefined rules and standards, minimizing errors and inconsistencies.
4. **Data Cleaning:** Data cleaning involves detecting and correcting errors, duplications, and inaccuracies in the data. This process ensures that the data is accurate, consistent, and ready for analysis.
5. **Data Transformation:** Data transformation is the process of converting raw data into a suitable format for further processing and analysis. It may involve data normalization, aggregation, or calculation of derived data.
6. **Data Storage:** Processed data is stored in databases or data warehouses for easy retrieval and future use. Proper data indexing and structuring facilitate efficient data retrieval and manipulation.
7. **Data Analysis:** Data analysis involves using various techniques and tools to extract insights, trends, patterns, and relationships from the processed data. Data analysis is crucial for generating meaningful information and supporting decision-making.
8. **Data Presentation:** The analyzed data is presented in a comprehensible format, such as reports, charts, graphs, dashboards, or visualizations. Effective data presentation enhances understanding and facilitates decision-making.
9. **Data Security:** Ensuring data security is fundamental in data

processing. Proper measures, such as encryption, access controls, and backups, protect data from unauthorized access, loss, or corruption.

10. **Data Privacy:** Data privacy is concerned with protecting the confidentiality and sensitive information of individuals or entities. Compliance with data protection regulations is essential in data processing.
11. **Real-time Data Processing:** In some cases, data processing needs to be performed in real-time or near-real-time, enabling immediate responses to changing conditions or events.
12. **Batch Processing:** Batch processing involves processing a large volume of data at once, typically during non-peak hours, to minimize system load and optimize processing efficiency.
13. **Data Integration:** Data integration is the process of combining data from multiple sources to create a unified view. This enables better analysis and decision-making by eliminating data silos.
14. **Data Governance:** Data governance establishes policies, processes, and responsibilities for managing data throughout its lifecycle to ensure its quality, integrity, and proper usage.

Data processing is a fundamental aspect of modern information systems, business intelligence, data analytics, and artificial intelligence. Mastering the fundamentals of data processing is essential for organizations to harness the power of data and derive valuable insights that drive business growth and innovation.

2.4 Computer Operation of Manual Information System

The computer operation of a manual information system involves leveraging computer technology to enhance and automate certain aspects of the manual processes. In a manual information system, data and information are processed and managed using physical paperwork, documents, and manual procedures. Integrating computer technology into such a system can bring several advantages, including increased efficiency, accuracy, and accessibility of information. Here's how computer operation can be applied to a manual information system:

1. **Data Entry and Storage:** Instead of manually writing and storing data on physical paper, computers can be used to input data digitally. This can be done through keyboard input, scanning documents, or using electronic forms. The data is then stored in computer databases or electronic files, allowing for easier retrieval and manipulation.
2. **Data Processing:** Computers can perform various data processing tasks faster and more accurately than manual methods. This includes calculations, sorting, filtering, and summarizing data. Computer software like spreadsheets can handle complex data processing tasks efficiently.
3. **Data Analysis and Reporting:** With computer software, data analysis and reporting become more robust and dynamic. Advanced analytical tools and software can generate meaningful insights and visualizations from large datasets, facilitating decision-making.
4. **Communication and Collaboration:** Computers enable seamless communication and collaboration among different users and departments within the organization. Email, instant messaging, and collaboration platforms streamline communication and information sharing.
5. **Automated Workflows:** Computers can be programmed to automate certain tasks and workflows. For example, an automated reminder system can notify users of pending tasks or deadlines.
6. **Document Management:** Computer-based document management systems allow for the organization, storage, and

retrieval of electronic documents. This eliminates the need for physical file cabinets and simplifies document search and version control.

7. **Security and Access Control:** Computers offer better security options, such as password protection and encryption, to safeguard sensitive information. Access to data and information can be controlled based on user roles and permissions.
8. **Backup and Recovery:** Regular data backups can be performed to protect against data loss due to hardware failures or other unforeseen events. Computer-based backup solutions offer more reliability than manual backups.
9. **Integration with External Systems:** Computers allow for integration with other systems and applications, such as customer relationship management (CRM) software, finance systems, and inventory management tools. This integration streamlines data sharing and eliminates the need for duplicate data entry.
10. **Scalability:** Computer systems can handle a large volume of data and grow as the organization's needs expand. This scalability ensures that the information system can accommodate future growth and changes.

While introducing computer operation to a manual information system can bring significant benefits, it's essential to plan and manage the transition carefully. Proper training, change management, and data migration strategies are crucial to ensure a smooth and successful adoption of computer technology in the organization's information management processes.

2.5 Components of Computer Systems

Computer systems consist of various interconnected components that work together to process data, perform tasks, and execute instructions. These components can be categorized into two main groups: hardware and software. Here are the key components of computer systems:

Hardware Components:

- **Central Processing Unit (CPU):** The CPU is the brain of the computer. It performs arithmetic and logical operations, executes instructions, and controls the overall operation of the computer.
- **Memory (RAM and ROM):** RAM (Random Access Memory) is the temporary storage used to hold data and program instructions that the CPU is currently processing. ROM (Read-Only Memory) contains essential firmware and instructions that are not modified during normal operation.
- **Storage Devices:** These include hard disk drives (HDDs), solid-state drives (SSDs), optical drives, and removable media (USB drives). They are used for long-term storage of data, programs, and files.
- **Input Devices:** Input devices allow users to input data and commands into the computer system. Common examples include keyboards, mice, touchscreens, scanners, and microphones.
- **Output Devices:** Output devices display or produce the results of computer processing. Examples include monitors, printers, speakers, and projectors.
- **Motherboard:** The motherboard is the main circuit board

that connects and allows communication between various hardware components of the computer.

- **Graphics Processing Unit (GPU):** The GPU is responsible for rendering graphics and images. It is essential for visual tasks such as gaming, video playback, and graphics-intensive applications.
- **Power Supply Unit (PSU):** The PSU provides electrical power to all components of the computer.
- **Cooling System:** Cooling systems, such as fans or liquid cooling, prevent the computer from overheating during intensive operations.

Software Components:

- **Operating System (OS):** The OS is the core software that manages the computer's hardware and software resources. It provides a user interface, manages memory, and handles system tasks.
- **Applications:** Applications are software programs that perform specific tasks or functions, such as word processing, web browsing, video editing, and gaming.
- **Utilities:** Utilities are software tools that perform various maintenance and optimization tasks, such as antivirus software, disk defragmentation, and backup software.
- **Device Drivers:** Device drivers are software components that enable communication between the operating system and hardware devices.
- **Firmware:** Firmware is a type of software embedded in hardware devices to control their operation.
- **Programming Languages:** Programming languages are used to write software code that instructs the computer to perform

specific tasks.

- **Middleware:** Middleware is software that connects different software applications or systems to facilitate communication and data exchange.
- **Web Browsers:** Web browsers are specialized applications that allow users to access and navigate the internet.

THE SEAMLESS INTERACTION between these hardware and software components enables computers to process data, run applications, and perform a wide range of tasks for various applications and industries.

2.6 Flow Chart, and Conversion of Manual to Computer Based Systems

Flow Chart:

A FLOWCHART IS A GRAPHICAL representation of a process or algorithm using different symbols and arrows to illustrate the sequence of steps and decision points. It helps visualize the flow of information or actions within a system, making complex processes more understandable. Flow charts are widely used in various fields, including software development, business process analysis, problem-solving, and project management.

Here are the common symbols used in flow charts:

1. **Start/End Symbol:** Represented by an oval shape, this symbol indicates the beginning and end points of the flowchart.
2. **Process Symbol:** A rectangular shape represents a specific action or task in the process. It describes the operation that is performed at that particular step.
3. **Decision Symbol:** Represented by a diamond shape, this

symbol denotes a decision point where a question is asked, and the flow can diverge based on different conditions.

4. **Connector Symbol:** A small, circular shape is used to connect different parts of the flowchart that are not directly connected by arrows.
5. **Input/Output Symbol:** A parallelogram shape represents input or output operations, such as reading data from a user or displaying information to the user.
6. **Connector Lines (Arrows):** Arrows are used to show the flow or direction of the process from one step to another. They indicate the sequence in which the steps are performed.

Flow charts provide a clear and concise representation of a process, making it easier to identify bottlenecks, inefficiencies, or potential errors. They serve as valuable tools for process documentation, analysis, and communication.

Conversion of Manual to Computer-Based Systems:

CONVERTING A MANUAL system to a computer-based system involves transitioning from traditional manual processes to using computer technology to streamline and enhance operations. Here are the key steps involved in this conversion:

1. **Assessment and Planning:**
    - **Assess the Current Manual System**: Understand the existing manual processes, including data collection, storage, and workflow.
    - **Identify Pain Points**: Identify the limitations and inefficiencies of the manual system that can be addressed through computerization.
    - **Define Objectives**: Determine the goals and

objectives of the computer-based system, such as improved efficiency, accuracy, and accessibility.

- **Plan the Conversion**: Create a detailed plan outlining the tasks, timeline, resources required, and roles and responsibilities for the conversion process.

2. **Data Collection and Digitization:**
    - **Gather Data**: Collect all relevant data used in the manual system.
    - **Data Entry and Digitization**: Input the collected data into the computer system.
3. **Software Selection and Customization:**
    - **Choose Software**: Select appropriate software applications that best meet the organization's needs, such as accounting software, inventory management systems, etc.
    - **Customize the Software**: Configure the chosen software to align with the organization's specific requirements.
4. **Data Integration and Testing:**
    - **Integrate Data**: Integrate the digitized data into the selected software.
    - **System Testing**: Conduct thorough testing to ensure the computer-based system functions as expected.
5. **User Training:**
    - **Train Users**: Provide comprehensive training to employees who will be using the computer-based system.
6. **Parallel Run and Transition:**
    - **Parallel Run**: Run both the manual and computer-based systems simultaneously for validation.
    - **Full Transition**: After successful parallel running, transition completely to the computer-based system.

7. **Monitoring and Support:**
    - **Monitor Performance**: Continuously monitor the computer-based system to ensure it meets the organization's objectives.
    - **Provide Support**: Offer ongoing support and assistance to users.
8. **Data Backup and Security:**
    - **Implement Data Backup**: Establish a data backup and recovery system.
    - **Ensure Data Security**: Implement security measures to safeguard sensitive information.
9. **Continuous Improvement:**
    - **Gather Feedback**: Seek feedback from users to identify areas for improvement.
    - **Continuously Upgrade**: Regularly update and upgrade the computer-based system.

By converting from a manual to a computer-based system, organizations can improve efficiency, accuracy, and data management while streamlining processes and making better-informed decisions.

2.7 Computer Systems Software, Application Software, and Telecommunication Modem

Computer Systems Software:

COMPUTER SYSTEMS SOFTWARE, also known as system software, refers to a group of programs designed to manage and control the hardware components and resources of a computer system. It acts as an intermediary between the hardware and application software, facilitating the smooth operation of the computer. The main types of computer systems software include:

- **Operating System (OS):** The operating system is the core system software that manages the computer's resources, such as memory, processors, storage, and input/output devices. It provides a user-friendly interface for users to interact with the computer and runs applications.
- **Device Drivers:** Device drivers are software components that enable communication between the operating system and specific hardware devices, such as printers, graphics cards, and network adapters. They allow the OS to control and utilize the hardware effectively.
- **Firmware:** Firmware is software that is embedded in hardware devices. It provides low-level control and instructions to the hardware. Firmware is typically stored in read-only memory (ROM) and is not easily modifiable by users.
- **BIOS/UEFI:** The Basic Input/Output System (BIOS) or Unified Extensible Firmware Interface (UEFI) is firmware that initializes and boots up the computer when it is powered on. It performs hardware diagnostics and provides a basic interface for configuring hardware settings before the operating system takes over.

Application Software:

APPLICATION SOFTWARE, also known as applications or apps, are programs designed to perform specific tasks or applications for users. Unlike system software, application software serves the needs of end-users and helps them complete various tasks. Examples of application software include:

- **Word Processing Software:** Programs like Microsoft Word or Google Docs that are used to create, edit, and format documents.
- **Spreadsheet Software:** Applications like Microsoft Excel or Google Sheets that are used for numerical calculations, data analysis, and creating graphs and charts.
- **Web Browsers:** Software like Google Chrome, Mozilla Firefox, or Microsoft Edge used to access and browse the internet.
- **Email Clients:** Programs like Microsoft Outlook or Mozilla Thunderbird used for sending, receiving, and managing emails.
- **Graphics and Image Editing Software:** Applications like Adobe Photoshop or GIMP used for editing and manipulating images and graphics.
- **Media Players:** Software like VLC Media Player or Windows Media Player used for playing audio and video files.

Telecommunication Modem:

A TELECOMMUNICATION modem, or simply a modem, is a hardware device used to modulate and demodulate digital signals to enable data transmission over communication channels. The word "modem" is derived from the term "modulator-demodulator." Modems are essential for transmitting digital data over analog communication mediums like telephone lines. They convert digital data from a computer or network into analog signals for transmission and then convert incoming analog signals back into digital data for reception. Modems are commonly used for internet connectivity, connecting to the internet service provider (ISP) over telephone lines (DSL modems) or cable lines (cable modems). With the widespread adoption of broadband internet technologies, traditional dial-up modems have become less common, but they still play a vital role in specific scenarios where high-speed internet is not available.

UNIT-3 DECISION MAKING

LESSON OUTLINE-

- ❖ DECISION MAKING
- ❖ Managerial Decision Making,
- ❖ Characteristics and components of Decision Support System.
- ❖ System Design Consideration,
- ❖ Input/Output Design, Forms Design,
- ❖ File Organization And Database,
- ❖ Data Management, File Design,
- ❖ Program Design, Control And Security

3.1 Introduction:

Decision making is the process of selecting the best course of action among several alternatives to achieve a specific goal or solve a problem. It is a fundamental cognitive process used by individuals, groups, and organizations to make choices and take actions based on available information and the evaluation of potential outcomes. Decision making can be influenced by various factors, including personal preferences, values, emotions, and external circumstances. The process of decision making typically involves the following steps:

1. **Identifying the Decision:**

- Clearly define the decision that needs to be made. Understand the problem or the goal that requires a decision.

2. **Gathering Information:**
    - Collect relevant data and information related to the decision. This may involve conducting research, analyzing past trends, or seeking expert opinions.
3. **Identifying Alternatives:**
    - Generate various possible alternatives or options that could be considered to address the problem or achieve the goal.
4. **Evaluating Alternatives:**
    - Assess the pros and cons of each alternative. Consider the potential outcomes, risks, benefits, and feasibility of each option.
5. **Making the Decision:**
    - Based on the information and analysis, choose the best alternative that aligns with the desired goals and objectives.
6. **Implementing the Decision:**
    - Put the chosen alternative into action. This may involve assigning tasks, allocating resources, and creating an action plan.
7. **Monitoring and Evaluating the Outcome:**
    - Continuously monitor the results of the decision. Evaluate whether the chosen alternative is achieving the desired results.
8. **Feedback and Adjustment:**
    - Based on the outcome, gather feedback and make any necessary adjustments or corrections to improve future decision making.

There are various models and approaches to decision making, including rational decision-making models, bounded rationality models, and intuitive decision-making models. The choice of a specific approach depends on the complexity of the decision, the available information, and the decision maker's cognitive abilities and preferences.

Factors that can influence decision making include cognitive biases, emotional states, individual values, social and cultural norms, time constraints, and the level of risk involved. Effective decision making requires critical thinking, analytical skills, problem-solving abilities, and the ability to weigh the potential consequences of different choices.

In organizational settings, decision making can involve individuals, teams, or management structures, depending on the nature and significance of the decision. Strategic decisions involve long-term planning and have a significant impact on the organization, while operational decisions deal with day-to-day tasks and processes. Effective decision making is crucial for individual success, organizational efficiency, and achieving desired outcomes in personal and professional contexts.

3.2 Managerial Decision Making

Managerial decision making refers to the process through which managers at various levels of an organization make choices and take actions to achieve organizational goals and solve problems. As decision-makers, managers are responsible for making informed and effective choices that can have a significant impact on the organization's performance, efficiency, and success. Managerial decision making involves a structured and systematic approach, considering both the internal and external factors that influence the decision.

Key aspects of managerial decision making include:

1. **Identifying the Problem or Opportunity:** Managers begin by identifying issues or opportunities that require attention or action. This could involve addressing operational challenges, exploring growth opportunities, responding to market changes, or improving organizational performance.
2. **Gathering Information and Data Analysis:** Managers collect relevant data and information to understand the problem fully. This may involve conducting research, analyzing market trends, studying financial reports, and seeking input from various sources.
3. **Defining Decision Criteria:** Managers establish criteria that the potential solutions must meet to be considered viable. These criteria could include financial feasibility, alignment with organizational goals, legal and ethical considerations, and potential risks and benefits.
4. **Generating Alternatives:** Managers brainstorm and create various alternative solutions to address the identified problem or opportunity. They encourage creativity and diverse perspectives to explore a wide range of options.
5. **Evaluating Alternatives:** Managers assess the advantages and disadvantages of each alternative against the decision criteria. They may use analytical tools, cost-benefit analysis, risk assessment, and other techniques to evaluate the potential outcomes.
6. **Selecting the Best Alternative:** Based on the evaluation, managers choose the most appropriate and feasible alternative that best aligns with the organization's objectives and constraints.
7. **Implementing the Decision:** Managers put the selected alternative into action by developing an implementation plan, allocating resources, and assigning responsibilities.
8. **Monitoring and Feedback:** Managers continuously monitor

the results of the decision and gather feedback. They assess whether the decision is producing the desired outcomes and if adjustments are needed.

9. **Learning from Outcomes:** Regardless of the decision's success, managers learn from the outcomes to improve future decision making. They use insights gained from past experiences to enhance their decision-making capabilities.
10. **Involvement of Stakeholders:** In complex decisions, managers may involve stakeholders from various levels and functions within the organization to gain diverse perspectives and achieve buy-in for the decision.

Effective managerial decision making requires a combination of analytical skills, critical thinking, problem-solving abilities, emotional intelligence, and the ability to consider both short-term and long-term consequences. The decision-making process may vary in complexity and time frame, ranging from routine operational decisions to strategic decisions with long-term implications.

A manager's ability to make well-informed decisions can significantly impact organizational performance, employee morale, and the achievement of strategic objectives. Therefore, developing strong decision-making skills is essential for successful management in any organization.

3.3 Characteristics and components of Decision Support System

A Decision Support System (DSS) is an interactive computer-based information system that assists individuals and organizations in making better decisions by providing data analysis, modeling, and decision-making tools. DSS is designed to support complex and semi-structured decision-making tasks, allowing users to explore and analyze information from different angles and scenarios.

Here are the key characteristics and components of a Decision Support System:

Characteristics of Decision Support System:

1. **Interactivity:** DSS is interactive and user-driven, allowing decision-makers to manipulate data, conduct analysis, and explore various scenarios based on their specific needs.
2. **Flexibility:** DSS is flexible and adaptable to different decision-making situations. It can accommodate changes in data inputs, assumptions, and decision models.
3. **Support for Semi-Structured Decisions:** DSS is particularly useful for semi-structured decisions that involve both structured and unstructured elements, where the problem is not fully defined, and there may be multiple possible solutions.
4. **Data Integration:** DSS integrates data from various sources and formats to provide decision-makers with a comprehensive view of the information relevant to the decision.
5. **Analytical Capabilities:** DSS provides powerful analytical tools for data analysis, statistical modeling, forecasting, and simulation to aid in decision-making.
6. **Modeling and What-If Analysis:** DSS allows users to create decision models and perform "what-if" analysis to assess the impact of different scenarios on the outcomes.
7. **User-Friendly Interface:** DSS is designed with a user-friendly interface to make it accessible and easy for non-technical users to interact with the system.
8. **Rapid Response Time:** DSS is designed to provide quick responses to queries and analysis, enabling decision-makers to make timely decisions.

Components of Decision Support System:

1. **Database Management System (DBMS):** The DBMS component stores and manages the data used in the decision-making process. It allows users to retrieve, manipulate, and update data efficiently.
2. **Model Base Management System (MBMS):** The MBMS component manages and stores different decision models and analytical tools used within the DSS.
3. **User Interface:** The user interface provides an interactive platform for decision-makers to interact with the DSS. It allows users to input data, perform analysis, and view results.
4. **Data Analysis Tools:** This component includes various data analysis tools, such as query tools, reporting tools, and data visualization tools, to explore and analyze data.
5. **Modeling Tools:** Modeling tools enable users to build mathematical, statistical, or simulation models to represent the decision-making problem.
6. **Knowledge-Based Management System (KBMS):** The KBMS component incorporates expert knowledge and rules that help guide decision-makers and provide suggestions or recommendations.
7. **Communication Network:** DSS often utilizes communication networks to access data from various sources, collaborate with other users, and share results.
8. **User Documentation and Help:** User documentation and help resources provide guidance on using the DSS effectively and understanding its functionalities.
9. **Security and Access Control:** DSS incorporates security measures to ensure that sensitive data and decision models are protected from unauthorized access.
10. **Feedback and Learning Mechanism:** Some DSS includes a

feedback loop that allows users to evaluate the outcomes of decisions and learn from past experiences to improve future decision-making processes.

DECISION SUPPORT SYSTEMS have become indispensable tools for organizations and decision-makers across various domains. They aid in solving complex problems, improving decision quality, and enhancing the overall effectiveness of decision-making processes.

3.4 System design consideration, input/ output design, forms design

System Design Consideration:

SYSTEM DESIGN IS THE process of defining the architecture, components, modules, interfaces, and data for a system to meet specified requirements. When designing a system, several key considerations should be taken into account:

1. **User Requirements:** Understand and analyze the needs and expectations of users to ensure the system aligns with their specific requirements.
2. **Scalability:** Design the system with the ability to handle increasing data volumes, user loads, and future expansions without significant rework.
3. **Reliability and Availability:** Ensure the system is reliable and available when needed, minimizing downtime and disruptions.
4. **Security:** Implement security measures to protect the system and its data from unauthorized access, breaches, and cyber-attacks.
5. **Performance:** Optimize the system's performance to achieve fast response times and efficient resource utilization.

6. **Integration:** Consider how the system will integrate with other existing systems, databases, or third-party applications.
7. **Usability and User Experience:** Design an intuitive and user-friendly interface to enhance user experience and ease of system use.
8. **Maintainability and Upgradability:** Make the system easy to maintain and update, ensuring it remains relevant and effective over time.
9. **Cost and Budget Constraints:** Consider budget limitations and cost-effectiveness in the design process.
10. **Compliance and Regulations:** Ensure the system complies with relevant industry standards, laws, and regulations.

Input/Output Design:

INPUT AND OUTPUT DESIGN refers to the process of determining how data will be entered into the system and how information will be presented to users. Considerations for input/output design include:

1. **Input Methods:** Choose appropriate input methods, such as keyboard, mouse, touchscreens, scanners, or voice recognition, based on user preferences and system requirements.
2. **Data Validation:** Implement validation checks to ensure data entered by users is accurate and consistent.
3. **Data Entry Controls:** Incorporate controls like drop-down menus, radio buttons, and checkboxes to streamline data entry and reduce errors.
4. **Error Handling:** Design clear and informative error messages to guide users when input errors occur.
5. **Output Formats:** Decide on the format of the output, such as reports, charts, graphs, or visualizations, based on the type of

data and user needs.

6. **Customization:** Provide options for users to customize output views according to their preferences.
7. **Printing and Displaying:** Consider the layout and formatting for printed reports and on-screen displays to ensure readability and clarity.
8. **Response Times:** Optimize the response times for input and output operations to enhance user experience.
9. **Multilingual Support:** If applicable, design the system to support multiple languages and character sets.

Forms Design:

FORMS DESIGN INVOLVES creating user interfaces that allow users to input data into the system. Considerations for forms design include:

1. **Layout and Organization:** Organize form elements in a logical and intuitive manner to guide users through the data entry process.
2. **Field Labels:** Provide clear and descriptive labels for each input field to indicate what information is required.
3. **Input Fields:** Choose appropriate input fields (textboxes, dropdowns, checkboxes, etc.) based on the type of data being entered.
4. **Required Fields:** Indicate mandatory fields and use validation to ensure users fill them out.
5. **Error Handling:** Clearly indicate any validation errors or missing information and provide instructions to correct them.
6. **Consistency:** Maintain consistent design elements, fonts, colors, and styles throughout the forms.
7. **Responsive Design:** Ensure the forms are responsive and accessible on various devices, including desktops, tablets, and

smartphones.

8. **Guidance and Help:** Include tooltips or contextual help to assist users in filling out the form correctly.
9. **Data Formatting:** Format data fields, such as dates, phone numbers, and postal codes, to match the expected format.
10. **Aesthetics:** Pay attention to visual design and aesthetics to create a pleasant and engaging user experience.

Effective system design consideration, input/output design, and forms design are crucial for building user-friendly, efficient, and reliable systems that meet the needs of users and contribute to the success of the organization.

3.5 File Organization And Database, Data Management

File Organization and Database:

FILE ORGANIZATION: File organization refers to the way data is stored and structured within files in a computer system. In file-based systems, data is organized into files and directories, and each file may contain records with related information. Common file organization methods include:

1. **Sequential File Organization:** Records are stored in sequential order, and accessing a specific record requires scanning through the file from the beginning until the desired record is found.
2. **Indexed File Organization:** An index is created to map the location of records in the file. The index allows for faster access to specific records without the need to scan the entire file.
3. **Random File Organization:** Records are stored in no particular order, and each record is assigned a unique

identifier or key. This method allows direct access to records based on their keys.

File organization has limitations in terms of data retrieval efficiency, data redundancy, and data consistency. As data and applications grow more complex, file-based systems are often replaced by database management systems (DBMS).

Database Management System (DBMS):

A DATABASE MANAGEMENT System (DBMS) is software that provides an interface between users and the database. It allows users to define, create, manipulate, and retrieve data from databases. DBMS offers several advantages over file-based systems, including:

1. **Data Independence:** DBMS provides data independence, separating the logical structure of data from the physical storage, making it easier to modify and maintain the database without affecting applications.
2. **Data Integrity and Security:** DBMS ensures data integrity through validation rules and provides mechanisms for controlling access and maintaining data security.
3. **Data Consistency:** DBMS enforces data consistency by allowing data to be updated in a controlled and coordinated manner.
4. **Data Abstraction:** DBMS provides data abstraction, allowing users to work with high-level conceptual data models rather than dealing with low-level storage details.
5. **Concurrent Access and Recovery:** DBMS supports concurrent access to data by multiple users and ensures data recovery in case of system failures.
6. **Data Query and Reporting:** DBMS allows users to perform complex queries, generate reports, and analyze data efficiently.

7. **Scalability and Performance:** DBMS is designed to handle large volumes of data and provides optimizations for efficient data retrieval and storage.

Data Management:

DATA MANAGEMENT ENCOMPASSES all processes and activities involved in the collection, storage, organization, retrieval, and utilization of data. It includes data governance, data quality, data security, and data integration. Key aspects of data management include:

1. **Data Collection:** Gathering data from various sources, such as applications, sensors, users, and external systems.
2. **Data Storage and Organization:** Storing data in databases or other data storage systems in a structured and organized manner.
3. **Data Cleaning and Quality Control:** Ensuring data accuracy, consistency, and completeness through data cleaning and validation processes.
4. **Data Integration:** Combining data from multiple sources to create a unified and coherent view of the data.
5. **Data Security:** Implementing measures to protect data from unauthorized access, data breaches, and cyber threats.
6. **Data Governance:** Establishing policies, procedures, and guidelines for data management to ensure data compliance and proper usage.
7. **Data Backup and Recovery:** Implementing regular data backups and recovery mechanisms to protect against data loss.
8. **Data Analysis and Insights:** Using data analytics tools and techniques to derive meaningful insights and knowledge from the data.

Effective data management is crucial for organizations to leverage data as a strategic asset, make informed decisions, and gain a competitive advantage in the digital age. A well-designed database management system plays a vital role in facilitating efficient data management and ensuring data is accessible, secure, and of high quality.

3.6 File Design, Program Design, Control And Security

File Design:

FILE DESIGN IS THE process of structuring and organizing data within files in a way that optimizes data storage, retrieval, and manipulation. Effective file design is crucial for efficient data management and smooth functioning of applications. Key considerations in file design include:

1. **Data Organization:** Determine the structure and format of data records within files, including field types, lengths, and relationships.
2. **File Organization Method:** Choose the appropriate file organization method (sequential, indexed, random) based on the application's data access requirements.
3. **Record Key:** Select a unique and meaningful record key that facilitates fast data retrieval and ensures data integrity.
4. **Record Length and Blocking Factor:** Decide the record length and blocking factor to efficiently utilize storage space and minimize access time.
5. **Data Redundancy:** Minimize data redundancy to conserve storage space and prevent inconsistencies.
6. **Data Validation:** Implement data validation rules to ensure data accuracy and maintain data integrity.
7. **File Maintenance:** Plan for file maintenance operations like

record addition, deletion, and updating to keep data up-to-date.

8. **Backup and Recovery:** Establish strategies for file backup and recovery to safeguard data against data loss.

Program Design:

PROGRAM DESIGN INVOLVES creating a detailed plan for the development of computer programs that effectively solve a specific problem or fulfill a particular task. Effective program design ensures that the software meets the specified requirements and performs efficiently. Key steps in program design include:

1. **Problem Analysis:** Understand the problem or task requirements and analyze the input, output, and processing needs.
2. **Algorithm Development:** Create a step-by-step algorithm that outlines the logic and sequence of operations to achieve the desired results.
3. **Data Structures:** Design the data structures needed to store and manipulate data effectively.
4. **Flowchart or Pseudocode:** Create flowcharts or pseudocode to visually represent the program's logic and control flow.
5. **Modularization:** Break down the program into smaller modules or functions for better organization and maintainability.
6. **Input/Output Handling:** Plan how the program will handle input data and produce the required output.
7. **Error Handling:** Design error handling mechanisms to detect and handle runtime errors or exceptional conditions.
8. **Code Optimization:** Optimize the program code to improve performance and reduce resource consumption.

Control and Security:

CONTROL AND SECURITY are essential aspects of software development to ensure that programs and systems operate as intended and data remains protected from unauthorized access. Key considerations for control and security include:

1. **Access Control:** Implement mechanisms to control user access to data and system functionalities based on user roles and permissions.
2. **Authentication and Authorization:** Use authentication methods (e.g., passwords, multi-factor authentication) to verify users' identities, and grant appropriate authorization based on user roles.
3. **Data Encryption:** Implement encryption techniques to secure sensitive data, both during storage and transmission.
4. **Error Handling and Logging:** Incorporate error handling and logging mechanisms to capture and record errors and system activities for analysis and troubleshooting.
5. **Backup and Recovery:** Establish regular data backups and recovery procedures to ensure data can be restored in case of data loss or system failures.
6. **Security Testing:** Conduct security testing to identify vulnerabilities and weaknesses in the software and fix them before deployment.
7. **Compliance:** Ensure that the software adheres to relevant security standards, industry regulations, and data protection laws.
8. **Version Control:** Implement version control to manage code changes and maintain a history of program revisions.

Effective control and security measures are vital for protecting sensitive data, preventing unauthorized access, and ensuring the reliability and integrity of software systems. They are critical components in building robust and trustworthy software applications.

UNIT-4 ERP-INTRODUCTION

LESSON OUTLINE-

- ERP Introduction- Benefits, Origin,
- Evolution and Structure: Conceptual Model of ERP,
- The Evolution of ERP, the Structure of ERP.
- Business Process Reengineering,
- Data ware Housing,
- Data Mining, Online
- Analytic Processing (OLAP),
- Product Life Cycle Management (PLM), LAP,
- Supply chain Management

4.1 ERP- INTRODUCTION

ERP, which stands for Enterprise Resource Planning, is a comprehensive and integrated software system that is designed to streamline and automate various business processes within an organization. It provides a centralized and unified platform to manage and coordinate all the core functions and activities across different departments, divisions, and business units of an enterprise. ERP systems are widely used in businesses of all sizes, ranging from small and medium enterprises to large multinational corporations.

The primary goal of ERP is to facilitate efficient data flow and information sharing among various departments, leading to improved collaboration, productivity, and decision-making. By consolidating and standardizing data, ERP enables real-time access to critical information, allowing managers and executives to gain insights into the company's performance and make informed strategic decisions.

Key features of ERP systems include:

1. **Integration:** ERP integrates various business functions, such as finance, accounting, sales, inventory, procurement, human resources, manufacturing, and customer relationship management (CRM). This integration ensures data consistency and eliminates data duplication across different systems.
2. **Centralized Database:** ERP uses a single, centralized database that serves as the backbone of the system. This shared database allows different departments to access and update information in real-time, promoting data accuracy and eliminating data silos.
3. **Modularity:** ERP systems are often modular, allowing organizations to choose and implement the specific modules that align with their business requirements. Examples of modules include finance and accounting, supply chain management, manufacturing, sales, and human resources.
4. **Standardization:** ERP encourages standardized business processes and workflows, ensuring consistent practices throughout the organization. This standardization simplifies training, reduces errors, and enhances efficiency.
5. **Automation:** ERP automates repetitive and manual tasks, reducing the need for manual intervention and improving process efficiency.
6. **Reporting and Analytics:** ERP systems offer robust reporting and analytics capabilities, allowing users to generate various reports, perform data analysis, and gain insights into business performance.

7. **Scalability:** ERP systems are designed to accommodate the growth of a business. They can scale up to meet the changing needs of expanding organizations.

Implementing an ERP system can be a complex and resource-intensive process. It involves careful planning, data migration, customization, and user training. However, the benefits of ERP implementation are numerous, including enhanced operational efficiency, increased productivity, reduced operational costs, improved customer service, better inventory management, and improved decision-making based on real-time data.

Some well-known ERP software vendors include SAP, Oracle, Microsoft Dynamics, Infor, and NetSuite, among others. The choice of an ERP system depends on the specific needs and requirements of an organization, its industry, and its budget.

4.2 Benefits, Origin

Benefits of ERP:

IMPLEMENTING AN ERP system offers numerous benefits to organizations across different industries. Some of the key advantages of ERP include:

1. **Streamlined Processes:** ERP integrates various business functions, eliminating data silos and streamlining processes. This leads to improved efficiency and reduced manual effort.
2. **Real-time Information:** ERP provides real-time access to critical business data and insights, enabling better decision-making and faster response to changing market conditions.
3. **Data Accuracy and Consistency:** With a centralized database, ERP ensures data accuracy and consistency, reducing the risk of data errors and inconsistencies.

4. **Improved Collaboration:** ERP promotes better collaboration and communication among different departments, leading to enhanced teamwork and coordination.
5. **Enhanced Productivity:** By automating repetitive tasks, ERP frees up employees' time, allowing them to focus on more value-added activities, which can lead to increased productivity.
6. **Cost Savings:** ERP can help reduce operational costs by optimizing processes, eliminating redundancies, and improving resource utilization.
7. **Better Customer Service:** ERP systems with CRM modules enable organizations to manage customer interactions more effectively, leading to improved customer service and satisfaction.
8. **Regulatory Compliance:** ERP systems can help organizations comply with industry regulations and standards by providing tools to monitor and control processes.
9. **Business Insights:** ERP systems offer powerful reporting and analytics capabilities, allowing organizations to gain valuable insights into their operations and performance.
10. **Scalability:** ERP systems are scalable and can grow with the organization, accommodating changes in business requirements and increasing data volumes.

Origin of ERP:

THE CONCEPT OF ERP originated from the need to address inefficiencies in business processes and information management. The roots of ERP can be traced back to the 1960s and 1970s when Material Requirements Planning (MRP) systems were developed to manage manufacturing processes and inventory control. MRP focused on optimizing the flow of materials and managing production schedules based on demand.

In the 1980s, MRP systems evolved into Manufacturing Resource Planning (MRP II) systems, which expanded their scope to include other business functions like finance, human resources, and sales. MRP II sought to integrate different departments and provide a more comprehensive view of an organization's resources and operations.

The term "Enterprise Resource Planning" was coined in the early 1990s to describe software systems that aimed to integrate and manage an enterprise's resources across various functional areas. ERP systems became more prominent as businesses recognized the benefits of integrating data and processes, leading to improved efficiency and decision-making.

SAP, founded in 1972 in Germany, is often credited with popularizing ERP systems. The company released its first ERP software, SAP R/2, in the early 1980s. Since then, many other software vendors have entered the ERP market, offering a variety of ERP solutions tailored to different industries and organizational sizes.

Today, ERP has become an essential tool for businesses seeking to optimize their operations, gain a competitive edge, and adapt to the challenges of an ever-changing business landscape. The continuous advancement of technology, including cloud computing and mobile applications, has further enhanced the capabilities and accessibility of ERP systems for organizations worldwide.

4.3 Evolution and Structure

Evolution of ERP:

THE EVOLUTION OF ERP can be traced through several stages, each building upon the concepts and functionalities of its predecessors:

1. **Material Requirements Planning (MRP):** In the 1960s,

MRP systems were developed to manage manufacturing processes and inventory control. MRP focused on calculating the material requirements for production based on demand, lead times, and bill of materials.

2. **Manufacturing Resource Planning (MRP II):** In the 1980s, MRP II systems emerged, expanding the scope beyond materials management. MRP II integrated additional business functions like finance, human resources, and sales into the planning process, providing a more comprehensive view of an organization's resources.
3. **Enterprise Resource Planning (ERP):** The term "Enterprise Resource Planning" was coined in the early 1990s. ERP systems aimed to integrate all business processes and data across an enterprise, including manufacturing, finance, human resources, supply chain, sales, and more. ERP systems provided a centralized database and a common platform for data sharing and collaboration.
4. **Extended ERP (ERP II):** In the late 1990s and early 2000s, ERP evolved into Extended ERP or ERP II. This stage focused on expanding the scope of ERP to include supply chain management, customer relationship management (CRM), business intelligence, and e-commerce capabilities.
5. **Cloud ERP and Mobile ERP:** In recent years, ERP systems have evolved to embrace cloud computing, offering cloud-based deployment models. Cloud ERP provides greater flexibility, scalability, and accessibility for organizations. Additionally, mobile ERP applications have emerged, enabling users to access ERP functionality on smartphones and tablets.

Structure of ERP:

THE STRUCTURE OF AN ERP system is based on a modular approach, where different functional modules address specific business areas. Each module focuses on a particular business process and integrates with other modules to form a cohesive system. Common ERP modules include:

1. **Finance and Accounting:** Handles financial transactions, general ledger, accounts payable, accounts receivable, financial reporting, budgeting, and financial analytics.
2. **Human Resources (HR):** Manages employee information, payroll, benefits, performance evaluations, recruitment, training, and workforce planning.
3. **Supply Chain Management (SCM):** Covers procurement, inventory management, order processing, logistics, demand forecasting, and supplier management.
4. **Manufacturing:** Handles production planning, scheduling, shop floor control, material requirements planning (MRP), and quality control.
5. **Sales and Distribution:** Manages sales processes, customer orders, pricing, invoicing, and sales analytics.
6. **Customer Relationship Management (CRM):** Focuses on customer information, sales leads, marketing campaigns, customer support, and customer analytics.
7. **Project Management:** Manages project planning, resource allocation, task tracking, and project reporting.
8. **Business Intelligence (BI):** Provides tools for data analysis, reporting, and decision support, enabling users to extract insights from the data stored in the ERP system.

The structure of ERP allows organizations to select and implement specific modules based on their unique business needs and priorities.

The integration of these modules ensures data consistency, improved collaboration, and a holistic view of the organization's operations, leading to increased efficiency and better decision-making capabilities.

4.4 Conceptual Model of ERP

The conceptual model of an ERP (Enterprise Resource Planning) system represents a high-level abstraction of how the various components, modules, and processes within the ERP system interact and collaborate to manage an organization's resources and operations. It provides a visual representation of the system's architecture, data flow, and the relationships between different modules. The conceptual model serves as a blueprint for designing and implementing the ERP system to meet the organization's specific requirements.

The key components of the conceptual model of an ERP system include:

1. **Centralized Database:** At the core of the conceptual model lies a centralized and unified database that stores all the relevant data required to support various business functions. This database acts as the single source of truth and ensures data consistency across different modules.
2. **Modules:** The ERP system is divided into functional modules, each responsible for managing specific business processes. Common modules include finance and accounting, human resources, supply chain management, manufacturing, sales, customer relationship management (CRM), and more.
3. **Integration:** The conceptual model highlights the integration between different modules, enabling seamless data flow and information exchange across the organization. This integration ensures that data entered in one module is automatically reflected in related modules, eliminating data duplication and promoting real-time data visibility.

4. **User Interfaces:** The model includes user interfaces for each module, providing a way for users to interact with the ERP system. User interfaces are designed to be user-friendly, intuitive, and tailored to the needs of specific user roles within the organization.
5. **Data Flow and Workflows:** The conceptual model illustrates the flow of data and workflows between different modules and business processes. This includes data entry, data processing, data storage, and data retrieval.
6. **Reporting and Analytics:** The model incorporates reporting and analytics capabilities, allowing users to generate various reports, dashboards, and data visualizations to gain insights into business performance and make informed decisions.
7. **Security and Access Control:** The conceptual model considers security measures to control access to sensitive data and ensure that users have appropriate permissions based on their roles and responsibilities.
8. **Scalability and Flexibility:** The model accounts for the scalability and flexibility of the ERP system to accommodate the evolving needs of the organization as it grows and adapts to changing business requirements.
9. **External Integration:** ERP systems often interact with external systems, such as third-party applications, suppliers, customers, and business partners. The conceptual model may include interfaces and integration points with these external entities.

The conceptual model serves as a foundation for further development, customization, and implementation of the ERP system. It guides system architects, developers, and business analysts in understanding the overall structure and functionality of the ERP system, helping them align the ERP solution with the organization's business processes and objectives.

4.5 The Evolution Of ERP

The evolution of ERP (Enterprise Resource Planning) spans several decades, reflecting the changing needs of businesses and advancements in technology. The evolution can be divided into several stages, each representing significant milestones in the development of ERP systems:

1. **1960s - Material Requirements Planning (MRP):** The concept of ERP has its roots in Material Requirements Planning (MRP) systems, which emerged in the 1960s. MRP systems were designed to manage manufacturing processes and inventory control. They focused on calculating material requirements for production based on demand, lead times, and bill of materials.
2. **1970s - Manufacturing Resource Planning (MRP II):** In the 1970s, MRP II systems evolved from MRP systems. MRP II expanded beyond materials management and integrated additional business functions like finance, human resources, sales, and purchasing. MRP II aimed to provide a comprehensive view of an organization's resources and operations.
3. **1980s - Enterprise Resource Planning (ERP):** In the 1980s, the term "Enterprise Resource Planning" (ERP) was coined. ERP systems took the concept of MRP II to the next level by integrating all business processes and data across an enterprise. ERP systems provided a centralized database and a common platform for data sharing and collaboration, streamlining business operations.
4. **1990s - ERP Expansion and Consolidation:** The 1990s saw the rapid expansion of ERP systems, with more vendors entering the market. ERP solutions began offering additional functionalities beyond core modules, such as customer

relationship management (CRM), supply chain management (SCM), and business intelligence (BI). The market also experienced consolidation, with larger ERP vendors acquiring smaller ones.

5. **2000s - ERP II and Web-based ERP:** In the early 2000s, the concept of ERP II emerged, which focused on extending ERP systems to include supply chain optimization, customer-centric features, and integration with external stakeholders. Web-based ERP solutions gained popularity, allowing users to access ERP systems through web browsers, enabling remote access and mobility.
6. **2010s - Cloud ERP and Mobile ERP:** The 2010s saw a significant shift towards cloud-based ERP solutions. Cloud ERP provided greater flexibility, scalability, and cost-effectiveness, making ERP more accessible to organizations of all sizes. Additionally, mobile ERP applications became more prevalent, enabling users to access ERP functionalities on smartphones and tablets.
7. **2020s - Intelligent ERP:** In recent years, ERP systems have been incorporating emerging technologies such as artificial intelligence (AI), machine learning, and data analytics. Intelligent ERP leverages these technologies to automate tasks, enhance decision-making, and provide predictive insights, leading to more agile and data-driven organizations.

The evolution of ERP continues to be driven by ongoing advancements in technology, the changing business landscape, and the need for organizations to stay competitive and adapt to digital transformation. ERP systems have become integral to modern businesses, providing a foundation for efficient and data-driven operations, improved collaboration, and enhanced customer experiences. As technology continues to evolve, the future of ERP will likely involve further integration with emerging technologies and deeper alignment with business needs.

4.6 The Structure of ERP

The structure of an ERP (Enterprise Resource Planning) system is designed to facilitate the integration and management of various business functions and processes within an organization. The structure allows different modules and components of the ERP system to interact and collaborate seamlessly, providing a centralized and unified platform for data sharing, decision-making, and process automation. The typical structure of an ERP system includes the following components:

1. **Centralized Database:** At the core of the ERP system is a centralized database that stores all the relevant data required to support various business functions. This database serves as the single source of truth, ensuring data consistency and eliminating data duplication across different modules.
2. **Functional Modules:** ERP systems are divided into functional modules, with each module designed to manage specific business processes. Common functional modules include:
    - **Finance and Accounting**: Handles financial transactions, general ledger, accounts payable, accounts receivable, financial reporting, budgeting, and taxation.
    - **Human Resources (HR):** Manages employee information, payroll, benefits, performance evaluations, recruitment, training, and workforce planning.
    - **Supply Chain Management (SCM):** Covers

procurement, inventory management, order processing, logistics, demand forecasting, and supplier management.

- **Manufacturing:** Handles production planning, scheduling, shop floor control, material requirements planning (MRP), and quality control.
- **Sales and Distribution**: Manages sales processes, customer orders, pricing, invoicing, and sales analytics.
- **Customer Relationship Management (CRM):** Focuses on managing customer information, sales leads, marketing campaigns, customer support, and customer analytics.

3. **Integration Layer:** The ERP system includes an integration layer that facilitates data exchange and communication between different modules. This integration ensures that data entered in one module is automatically reflected in related modules, eliminating the need for redundant data entry and promoting real-time data visibility.
4. **User Interfaces:** Each functional module of the ERP system is equipped with user interfaces that allow users to interact with the system. User interfaces are designed to be user-friendly, intuitive, and tailored to the needs of specific user roles within the organization.
5. **Reporting and Analytics:** The ERP system incorporates reporting and analytics capabilities, enabling users to generate various reports, dashboards, and data visualizations to gain insights into business performance and make informed decisions.
6. **Security and Access Control:** The ERP system implements security measures to control access to sensitive data and ensure

that users have appropriate permissions based on their roles and responsibilities. This helps safeguard data from unauthorized access and potential security breaches.

7. **Scalability and Flexibility:** The ERP system is designed to be scalable and flexible, allowing it to adapt to the evolving needs of the organization as it grows and encounters changing business requirements.
8. **External Integration:** ERP systems often interact with external systems, such as third-party applications, suppliers, customers, and business partners. The ERP structure may include interfaces and integration points with these external entities to enable seamless data exchange.

The structure of an ERP system enables organizations to integrate their various business processes, optimize resource utilization, improve collaboration, and gain a holistic view of their operations. This integration helps organizations make more informed decisions, improve efficiency, and achieve their business objectives.

4.7 Business Process Reengineering

Business Process Reengineering (BPR) is a management approach that involves the radical redesign of an organization's core business processes to achieve significant improvements in performance, efficiency, and effectiveness. The goal of BPR is to fundamentally rethink and redesign how work is done to better align with the organization's strategic objectives and leverage emerging technologies.

Key principles and characteristics of Business Process Reengineering include:

1. **Process-Centric Focus:** BPR centers around the organization's processes rather than individual tasks or departments. It looks at end-to-end processes and how they

interact across different functions and departments.

2. **Radical Redesign:** BPR advocates making substantial and transformative changes to processes, often starting from a clean slate, rather than incremental improvements. It challenges the status quo and questions existing assumptions.
3. **Customer-Centric Approach:** BPR emphasizes meeting customer needs and delivering value to customers. The redesign aims to enhance customer satisfaction and create a more customer-centric organization.
4. **Simplification and Elimination of Non-Value-Adding Steps:** BPR seeks to eliminate non-essential steps and bureaucracy in processes, simplifying workflows to reduce delays and inefficiencies.
5. **Cross-Functional Teams:** BPR involves multidisciplinary teams with representatives from different departments, fostering collaboration and shared responsibility for process redesign.
6. **Technology Enablement:** BPR leverages technology to support and optimize redesigned processes. Automation, digitalization, and information systems play a crucial role in enabling process improvements.
7. **Performance Measurement:** BPR emphasizes the importance of measuring and monitoring process performance to identify bottlenecks, inefficiencies, and areas for further improvement.
8. **Focus on Results:** BPR is results-oriented, aiming for concrete improvements in key performance indicators, such as cost reduction, cycle time reduction, and improved customer satisfaction.

Business Process Reengineering is often pursued in situations where organizations are experiencing significant challenges, such as declining competitiveness, outdated processes, rising costs, or a need to respond to market changes. BPR can lead to several benefits, including:

1. **Improved Efficiency:** By eliminating redundant steps and streamlining processes, BPR can lead to faster and more efficient operations.
2. **Cost Reduction:** BPR can identify areas of cost inefficiency and help the organization achieve cost savings.
3. **Enhanced Customer Satisfaction:** Customer-centric process redesign can lead to improved service delivery and higher customer satisfaction.
4. **Innovation:** BPR encourages creative thinking and innovative solutions to address business challenges.
5. **Competitive Advantage:** Successful BPR can provide the organization with a competitive edge by enabling it to deliver value more effectively and efficiently.

However, Business Process Reengineering is a complex and challenging undertaking. It requires strong leadership, effective change management, and a willingness to break away from traditional ways of doing things. Moreover, BPR initiatives should be well-planned and involve stakeholders at all levels to ensure successful implementation and sustainable results.

4.8 Data ware Housing, Data Mining

Data Warehousing:

DATA WAREHOUSING IS a process of collecting, storing, organizing, and managing large volumes of structured and unstructured data from various sources to support business intelligence and analytics activities. The data is consolidated into a single repository known as a data warehouse, which is optimized for analytical processing and reporting.

Key characteristics of data warehousing include:

1. **Centralized Data Storage:** Data warehousing integrates data from different sources, such as transactional databases, spreadsheets, flat files, and external systems, into a centralized repository.
2. **ETL (Extract, Transform, Load):** ETL processes are used to extract data from source systems, transform it into a consistent format, and load it into the data warehouse.
3. **Data Cleansing and Integration:** Data warehousing involves data cleansing and integration to ensure data quality and consistency.
4. **Subject-Oriented:** Data in a data warehouse is organized around specific subject areas, such as sales, finance, inventory, or customer data, to facilitate business analysis.
5. **Time-Variant:** Data warehousing maintains historical data, allowing users to analyze trends and patterns over time.
6. **Non-Volatile:** Once data is loaded into the data warehouse, it is typically read-only and not subject to frequent updates or changes.

Data warehousing provides a foundation for business intelligence (BI) and analytics solutions, enabling organizations to perform complex queries, generate reports, create dashboards, and gain valuable insights from their data.

Data Mining:

DATA MINING IS THE process of discovering meaningful patterns, relationships, and insights from large datasets using various statistical and machine learning techniques. It involves the extraction of hidden, previously unknown, and potentially valuable information from data.

Key steps in the data mining process include:

1. **Data Exploration:** Understanding the data, its structure, and potential relationships to identify the appropriate data mining techniques.
2. **Data Preprocessing:** Cleaning and preparing the data to remove noise, handle missing values, and transform it into a suitable format for analysis.
3. **Data Mining Algorithms:** Applying various algorithms such as clustering, classification, regression, association rule mining, and anomaly detection to discover patterns in the data.
4. **Pattern Evaluation:** Assessing the discovered patterns and relationships to determine their relevance and usefulness for decision-making.
5. **Knowledge Presentation:** Presenting the results of data mining analysis in a meaningful and understandable manner to stakeholders.

Data mining is widely used across various industries for diverse applications, such as customer segmentation, fraud detection, market basket analysis, predictive maintenance, sentiment analysis, and recommendation systems.

Both data warehousing and data mining are integral components of the larger field of business intelligence and analytics. Data warehousing provides the foundation for storing and managing vast amounts of data, while data mining enables organizations to uncover valuable insights and patterns from that data, supporting informed decision-making and business strategies.

4.9 Online Analytic Processing (OLAP)

Online Analytic Processing (OLAP) is a category of software tools and technologies that enable users to interactively analyze and explore multidimensional data from various perspectives. OLAP systems are designed to facilitate complex and rapid data analysis for decision-making, reporting, and business intelligence purposes.

Key characteristics and features of OLAP include:

1. **Multidimensional Data Model:** OLAP organizes data into a multidimensional model, which allows users to view data from different dimensions or attributes simultaneously. Dimensions represent different categories or characteristics of data, and measures represent the numeric data that users want to analyze (e.g., sales, revenue, quantity).
2. **Cubes:** The central concept in OLAP is the data cube, also known as a hypercube or OLAP cube. A cube represents a multi-dimensional dataset, where each axis corresponds to a specific dimension, and the intersection of these axes contains the measure values. Cubes allow users to drill down or roll up the data, analyzing it at different levels of granularity.
3. **Slicing, Dicing, and Pivoting:** OLAP provides interactive tools for slicing (selecting specific data from a cube), dicing (breaking down a cube into smaller parts), and pivoting (rotating the cube to view data from different angles).
4. **Aggregation and Calculations:** OLAP supports fast aggregation and calculation of data, allowing users to perform calculations on the fly, such as sum, average, count, and percentages.
5. **Fast Response Time:** OLAP systems are designed to deliver rapid responses to queries and analysis, even with large and complex datasets.
6. **User-Friendly Interfaces:** OLAP tools offer user-friendly

interfaces, such as pivot tables, charts, and graphs, which make it easier for users to interact with and explore data intuitively.

7. **Drill-Down and Roll-Up:** OLAP enables users to drill down into detailed data or roll up to higher-level summaries, providing a multi-level view of information.
8. **Real-Time Data Updates:** Some OLAP systems support real-time data updates, allowing users to analyze data as it is being generated.

OLAP is commonly used in various business domains, including finance, sales, marketing, supply chain, and human resources. It enables users, such as managers, analysts, and decision-makers, to gain valuable insights from their data quickly and efficiently.

Types of OLAP systems:

1. **MOLAP (Multidimensional OLAP):** MOLAP systems store data in a multidimensional format, optimizing performance for fast query response times. Examples of MOLAP systems include Microsoft Analysis Services (part of Microsoft SQL Server) and IBM Cognos TM1.
2. **ROLAP (Relational OLAP):** ROLAP systems store data in relational databases and perform calculations on-the-fly during query execution. This allows ROLAP systems to handle larger datasets but may sacrifice some query performance compared to MOLAP. Examples of ROLAP systems include Microsoft SQL Server Analysis Services (Tabular model) and Oracle OLAP.

OLAP PLAYS A CRUCIAL role in business intelligence and decision support systems, empowering users to explore data from different perspectives, identify trends, make data-driven decisions, and gain a deeper understanding of business performance.

4.10 Product Life Cycle Management (PLM)

Product Life Cycle Management (PLM) is a strategic business approach that involves the management of a product or a portfolio of products throughout their entire life cycle, from conception and design through production, use, and disposal. PLM encompasses a set of processes, tools, and methodologies to optimize product development, improve collaboration, and enhance decision-making at every stage of the product's life.

The key stages of Product Life Cycle Management are:

1. **Concept:**
    - In the concept stage, ideas for new products or product improvements are generated and evaluated. Market research, customer feedback, and competitive analysis play a significant role in shaping product concepts.
2. **Design and Development:**
    - During this stage, the product's design is developed, considering factors such as functionality, manufacturability, and cost. Engineering teams work on prototypes and conduct testing to ensure the product meets requirements and standards.
3. **Manufacturing and Production:**
    - Once the product design is finalized, it moves into the manufacturing and production phase. PLM involves optimizing manufacturing processes, ensuring quality control, and managing the supply chain for efficient production.
4. **Introduction and Launch:**
    - The product is introduced to the market, and

marketing and sales efforts are focused on creating awareness and generating initial sales.

5. **Growth:**
   - In the growth stage, sales and market share start to increase as the product gains traction and acceptance in the market.
6. **Maturity:**
   - The product reaches its peak sales during the maturity stage. Competition may increase, and companies may focus on product differentiation and cost optimization.
7. **Decline:**
   - Sales begin to decline as the product reaches the end of its life cycle due to changes in the market, technology advancements, or shifting consumer preferences.
8. **End of Life and Disposal:**
   - The product is discontinued, and PLM includes considerations for product end-of-life management, such as recycling, disposal, or replacement strategies.

Benefits of Product Life Cycle Management include:

1. **Improved Product Development:** PLM helps streamline the product development process, reducing time to market and enhancing product quality.
2. **Enhanced Collaboration:** PLM encourages cross-functional collaboration among teams, enabling better communication and information sharing.
3. **Regulatory Compliance:** PLM ensures that products meet industry regulations and safety standards throughout their life cycle.
4. **Cost Reduction:** PLM helps identify areas for cost

optimization and waste reduction, leading to cost savings in product development and manufacturing.

5. **Greater Visibility:** PLM provides real-time visibility into the product's status, performance, and customer feedback, enabling data-driven decision-making.
6. **Sustainability and Environmental Considerations:** PLM incorporates environmental considerations, such as eco-design and product end-of-life management, to promote sustainability.

PLM software systems play a crucial role in supporting and automating PLM processes, managing product data, facilitating collaboration, and optimizing product-related activities. These systems centralize product information, support version control, and aid in managing changes throughout the product life cycle.

4.11 Supply Chain Management (SCM):

Supply Chain Management is the process of planning, executing, and controlling the efficient movement and storage of goods, services, and information from the point of origin to the point of consumption. It involves managing the entire network of organizations, resources, and activities that contribute to delivering products or services to end customers.

Key components and activities of Supply Chain Management include:

1. **Planning:** This involves strategic decision-making regarding sourcing, production, distribution, inventory levels, and demand forecasting.
2. **Sourcing:** Identifying and selecting suppliers, negotiating contracts, and managing relationships with vendors.
3. **Procurement:** Acquiring goods or services from suppliers to

meet production or distribution requirements.

4. **Production:** Manufacturing or assembling products based on demand forecasts and sales orders.
5. **Inventory Management:** Optimizing inventory levels to balance supply and demand while minimizing carrying costs.
6. **Distribution:** Managing the movement of goods from production facilities to distribution centers and eventually to retailers or end customers.
7. **Logistics and Transportation:** Selecting the most efficient transportation methods and managing the logistics network to ensure timely delivery.
8. **Information Management:** Utilizing advanced technologies and data analytics to capture and analyze supply chain data for better decision-making.
9. **Risk Management:** Identifying potential risks and implementing strategies to mitigate disruptions in the supply chain.
10. **Collaboration and Communication:** Establishing effective communication and collaboration between various stakeholders, including suppliers, manufacturers, distributors, and retailers.

Supply Chain Management is critical for organizations to achieve operational efficiency, cost savings, faster time-to-market, improved customer service, and a competitive advantage in the market. Effective SCM practices help businesses optimize their supply chain, reduce inventory costs, minimize lead times, and respond swiftly to changes in market demand.

By optimizing the entire supply chain, organizations can create a seamless flow of goods and information, reduce inefficiencies, and enhance overall customer satisfaction. SCM plays a crucial role in a company's success, especially in today's global and interconnected business environment.

UNIT-5 ERP DYNAMICS

LESSON OUTLINE-

- ERP Marketplace And Marketplace Dynamics: Market Overview, Marketplace Dynamics,
- The Changing ERP Market. ERP- Functional Modules:
- Introduction, Functional Modules Of ERP Software, IntegrationOf ERP,
- Supply Chain And Customer Relationship Applications

5.1 Introduction :

ERP Dynamics typically refers to "Microsoft Dynamics," which is a line of enterprise resource planning (ERP) and customer relationship management (CRM) software applications developed and marketed by Microsoft. Microsoft Dynamics offers a suite of integrated business applications that help organizations manage various aspects of their business operations, including finance, supply chain, sales, marketing, human resources, and customer service.

The main products in the Microsoft Dynamics family include:

1. **Microsoft Dynamics 365 Finance and Operations (formerly Dynamics AX):** This ERP application is designed

to handle financial management, supply chain management, manufacturing, retail, and other core business processes.

2. **Microsoft Dynamics 365 Business Central (formerly Dynamics NAV):** This ERP application is tailored for small and medium-sized businesses and covers financial management, sales, purchasing, inventory, and project management.
3. **Microsoft Dynamics 365 Customer Engagement (formerly Dynamics CRM):** This CRM application helps organizations manage their customer interactions, sales processes, marketing campaigns, and customer service operations.
4. **Microsoft Dynamics 365 Sales (formerly Dynamics 365 for Sales):** This application focuses specifically on sales force automation, lead management, and sales performance tracking.
5. **Microsoft Dynamics 365 Marketing (formerly Dynamics 365 for Marketing):** This application provides tools for planning, executing, and analyzing marketing campaigns.
6. **Microsoft Dynamics 365 Human Resources (formerly Dynamics 365 for Talent):** This application helps organizations manage their human resources processes, including recruitment, onboarding, employee records, and performance management.

Microsoft Dynamics offers cloud-based versions of these applications, allowing organizations to access and manage their data from anywhere through a web browser. Additionally, on-premises deployments are available for some of the applications for organizations that prefer to host their ERP or CRM systems locally.

One of the key advantages of Microsoft Dynamics is its seamless integration with other Microsoft products, such as Microsoft Office 365, SharePoint, and Power BI. This integration allows users to work with familiar tools and access relevant information across various business functions.

Microsoft Dynamics is widely used across industries and organizations of all sizes, providing a scalable and flexible solution for managing critical business processes and fostering growth and productivity.

5.2 ERP Marketplace and Marketplace Dynamics

ERP Marketplace refers to the ecosystem where various ERP (Enterprise Resource Planning) software solutions and related services are offered, bought, and sold. It includes a wide range of vendors, resellers, consultants, and service providers that offer ERP products and services to businesses looking to implement or upgrade their ERP systems.

Key components of the ERP Marketplace include:

1. **ERP Vendors:** These are companies that develop and sell ERP software solutions. ERP vendors create and maintain the software, provide technical support, and offer updates and new releases.
2. **Resellers and Implementation Partners:** Resellers and implementation partners are companies or individuals that work with ERP vendors to sell their products and provide implementation, customization, and support services to end-user organizations.
3. **Consultants and System Integrators:** ERP consultants and system integrators are professionals or firms that provide expert advice and services related to ERP selection, implementation, and optimization. They help businesses with the planning, configuration, and integration of ERP systems.
4. **Marketplace Platforms:** Some online platforms act as

marketplaces for ERP software, providing a space for ERP vendors, resellers, and buyers to connect and conduct transactions.

5. **Third-Party Add-ons and Extensions:** In the ERP Marketplace, third-party vendors may offer add-ons, extensions, or integrations to enhance the functionality of existing ERP systems, providing additional features and capabilities.
6. **ERP User Community:** The ERP Marketplace fosters a user community where organizations that have implemented ERP systems can share experiences, best practices, and insights with others considering ERP adoption.

Marketplace Dynamics in the ERP context refer to the various factors that influence the buying and selling of ERP software and services. These dynamics are continually evolving and can include:

1. **Technology Trends:** Advancements in technology, such as cloud computing, artificial intelligence, and data analytics, impact ERP software development and adoption.
2. **Competitive Landscape:** The competitive environment among ERP vendors and service providers affects pricing, features, and service offerings.
3. **Industry Specificity:** Some ERP solutions are tailored to specific industries, such as manufacturing, healthcare, retail, or finance, to address unique business needs.
4. **Customer Needs:** Customer requirements, pain points, and preferences drive ERP development and influence the types of solutions offered in the marketplace.
5. **Economic Factors:** Economic conditions, such as business growth, investment, or downturns, can influence ERP adoption rates and investment decisions.
6. **Regulatory Compliance:** Changes in regulatory

requirements may prompt organizations to seek ERP solutions that address compliance needs.

7. **Vendor Strategies:** ERP vendors' marketing and sales strategies, product roadmaps, and partnerships play a role in the marketplace dynamics.

Understanding marketplace dynamics is essential for businesses looking to select an ERP solution that aligns with their needs and objectives. By assessing marketplace dynamics, organizations can make informed decisions, negotiate better deals, and ensure a successful ERP implementation that meets their long-term business goals.

5.3 Market Overview, Marketplace Dynamics

Market Overview:

A MARKET OVERVIEW PROVIDES a snapshot of the current state of a specific market, offering insights into its size, growth, trends, competitive landscape, and key players. It helps businesses and stakeholders understand the broader market context and make informed decisions. Market overviews typically involve market research and analysis, incorporating data from various sources such as industry reports, market studies, surveys, and expert opinions.

The components of a market overview may include:

1. **Market Size:** The total value or volume of goods and services traded in the market within a specific timeframe.
2. **Market Growth:** The historical and projected growth rate of the market over time.
3. **Market Trends:** Notable patterns or changes in consumer behavior, technology, regulations, or industry practices.
4. **Market Segmentation:** How the market is divided into

different customer segments based on demographics, geographic locations, or other criteria.

5. **Competitive Landscape:** An analysis of the major players in the market, their market shares, strengths, weaknesses, and strategies.
6. **Key Market Drivers and Challenges:** Factors that influence market growth and potential obstacles that businesses may encounter.
7. **Regulatory Environment:** An assessment of regulations and policies that impact the market.
8. **Emerging Opportunities:** New areas or niches in the market that present growth prospects.

Marketplace Dynamics:

MARKETPLACE DYNAMICS refer to the forces, factors, and influences that shape the behavior of buyers and sellers in a market. Understanding marketplace dynamics is essential for businesses to develop effective strategies, respond to changes, and stay competitive. These dynamics are subject to continuous changes due to various internal and external factors, including economic conditions, technology advancements, consumer preferences, and industry trends.

Key elements of marketplace dynamics include:

1. **Supply and Demand:** The interaction between the availability of products or services (supply) and the desire of buyers to acquire them (demand) affects prices, sales, and market equilibrium.
2. **Competition:** The level of competition among businesses in the market influences pricing strategies, product differentiation, and market share.
3. **Innovation and Technology:** Technological advancements can disrupt existing markets, create new opportunities, and

change how products or services are delivered.

4. **Consumer Behavior:** Changes in consumer preferences, needs, and buying habits impact product development and marketing strategies.
5. **Regulatory Changes:** Shifts in government policies, regulations, or trade agreements can influence market conditions and business operations.
6. **Macroeconomic Factors:** Economic indicators like GDP growth, inflation rates, and unemployment impact overall market conditions.
7. **Globalization:** International trade and competition from global markets affect domestic industries and businesses.
8. **Industry Trends:** Emerging trends in the industry, such as sustainability, digitalization, or remote work, can shape market dynamics.

Analyzing marketplace dynamics helps businesses identify opportunities and threats, adapt to changing conditions, and make informed decisions about product development, marketing, pricing, and market entry strategies. By staying attuned to market dynamics, organizations can stay agile and competitive in an ever-evolving business landscape.

5.4 The Changing ERP Market

The ERP (Enterprise Resource Planning) market has been undergoing significant changes and transformations in recent years. These changes are driven by various factors, including technological advancements, shifting customer demands, evolving business requirements, and industry trends. Some of the key changes in the ERP market include:

1. **Cloud-Based Solutions:** One of the most significant shifts

in the ERP market is the rapid adoption of cloud-based ERP solutions. Cloud ERP offers benefits such as scalability, flexibility, cost-effectiveness, and easy accessibility from anywhere with an internet connection. Many businesses are moving away from traditional on-premises ERP systems in favor of cloud-based solutions.

2. **Focus on User Experience:** ERP vendors are now placing a greater emphasis on user experience and interface design. Modern ERP systems are designed to be more intuitive, user-friendly, and customizable, making them easier for employees to use and navigate.
3. **Mobile ERP:** With the increasing use of mobile devices, mobile ERP applications are becoming more prevalent. Mobile ERP enables users to access and interact with ERP functionalities on smartphones and tablets, allowing for real-time data access and decision-making on the go.
4. **Integration with Emerging Technologies:** ERP vendors are integrating emerging technologies such as artificial intelligence (AI), machine learning, internet of things (IoT), and analytics into their systems. These technologies enhance ERP capabilities, providing insights, automation, and predictive functionalities to improve decision-making and operational efficiency.
5. **Industry-Specific Solutions:** Many ERP vendors are developing industry-specific solutions tailored to the unique needs of different sectors, such as manufacturing, healthcare, retail, and professional services. These industry-focused ERP solutions offer specialized features and workflows that address specific industry challenges.
6. **Modular and Flexible Solutions:** Instead of monolithic ERP systems, vendors are offering more modular and flexible solutions. This allows businesses to choose and implement

only the modules they need, enabling a more tailored and cost-effective approach to ERP implementation.

7. **Data Security and Compliance:** As data breaches and cybersecurity threats increase, ERP vendors are placing greater emphasis on data security and compliance. Modern ERP systems include robust security measures to protect sensitive data and ensure compliance with data privacy regulations.
8. **Real-Time Analytics and Reporting:** ERP systems are now equipped with advanced analytics and reporting capabilities. Real-time data analytics allows businesses to gain immediate insights into their operations, enabling faster decision-making and proactive management.
9. **Integration with Other Business Applications:** ERP vendors are focusing on seamless integration with other business applications and software, such as CRM, supply chain management, e-commerce platforms, and human resource management systems. Integration simplifies data sharing and streamlines business processes.
10. **Subscription-Based Pricing:** The shift to cloud-based ERP has also led to a change in pricing models. Many ERP vendors offer subscription-based pricing, where businesses pay a regular fee for using the software, instead of upfront capital expenses.

These changes in the ERP market reflect the growing demand for modern, agile, and technologically advanced solutions that can adapt to the evolving needs of businesses in a fast-paced and digitalized world. Organizations are increasingly looking for ERP systems that can drive innovation, improve operational efficiency, and support data-driven decision-making to gain a competitive edge in their industries.

5.5 ERP- Functional Modules:

Introduction

ERP (Enterprise Resource Planning) systems are comprehensive software solutions that integrate various business processes and functions into a unified platform. These systems consist of multiple functional modules, each designed to address specific aspects of an organization's operations. Each module focuses on a specific business function and contains tools, features, and workflows to manage and optimize those processes. The integration of these modules allows data to flow seamlessly across different functions, providing a holistic view of the organization's operations.

Here is an introduction to some of the common functional modules found in ERP systems:

1. **Finance and Accounting Module:**
   - This module manages all financial transactions, including accounts payable (AP), accounts receivable (AR), general ledger, financial reporting, budgeting, and cash management. It helps organizations maintain accurate financial records and supports financial analysis and decision-making.
2. **Human Resources (HR) Module:**
   - The HR module handles all aspects of human resource management, including employee information, payroll processing, benefits administration, time and attendance tracking, performance evaluations, training, and recruitment. It helps streamline HR processes and ensures compliance with labor regulations.
3. **Supply Chain Management (SCM) Module:**
   - The SCM module oversees the flow of goods and services from suppliers to customers. It includes functions such as procurement, inventory

management, order processing, supplier management, demand forecasting, and logistics. Effective SCM optimizes the supply chain, reduces costs, and improves delivery times.

4. **Manufacturing Module:**
   - This module focuses on production planning, scheduling, shop floor control, material requirements planning (MRP), quality management, and product lifecycle management (PLM). It helps optimize manufacturing processes and ensures efficient production.
5. **Sales and Distribution Module:**
   - The sales and distribution module manages sales processes, customer orders, pricing, invoicing, and sales analytics. It enables sales teams to manage leads, opportunities, and customer interactions effectively.
6. **Customer Relationship Management (CRM) Module:**
   - The CRM module is dedicated to managing customer information, interactions, and relationships. It helps sales and marketing teams track leads, manage customer data, and improve customer service.
7. **Project Management Module:**
   - This module assists in project planning, resource allocation, task management, time tracking, and project cost control. It is beneficial for organizations that undertake projects with specific timelines and budgets.
8. **Asset Management Module:**
   - The asset management module handles the tracking, maintenance, and utilization of assets within the organization. It helps organizations optimize asset

performance and reduce downtime.

These are just a few examples of functional modules in an ERP system. The availability and complexity of modules may vary depending on the ERP vendor and the specific industry or organizational needs. ERP systems offer a comprehensive and integrated approach to managing business processes, allowing organizations to improve efficiency, reduce manual work, and make data-driven decisions across all aspects of their operations.

5.6 Functional Modules of ERP Software

ERP (Enterprise Resource Planning) software consists of a collection of functional modules, each catering to specific business functions. These modules are designed to work together, sharing data and information, to provide a seamless and integrated solution for managing various aspects of an organization's operations. The specific modules included in an ERP system may vary based on the software vendor and the industry focus. Here are some of the common functional modules found in ERP software:

1. **Finance and Accounting Module:**
    - This module manages financial transactions, general ledger, accounts payable (AP), accounts receivable (AR), fixed assets, financial reporting, and cash management. It helps organizations maintain accurate financial records and supports financial analysis and decision-making.
2. **Human Resources (HR) Module:**
    - The HR module handles human resource management processes, such as employee information, payroll processing, benefits administration, time and attendance tracking,

performance management, training, and recruitment. It streamlines HR processes and ensures compliance with labor regulations.

3. **Supply Chain Management (SCM) Module:**
    - The SCM module oversees the end-to-end supply chain, including procurement, inventory management, order processing, supplier management, demand forecasting, logistics, and distribution. It optimizes supply chain operations and improves collaboration with suppliers and customers.
4. **Manufacturing Module:**
    - This module focuses on production planning, scheduling, shop floor control, material requirements planning (MRP), quality management, product lifecycle management (PLM), and maintenance. It streamlines manufacturing processes and ensures efficient production.
5. **Sales and Distribution Module:**
    - The sales and distribution module manages sales processes, customer orders, pricing, quotations, sales analytics, and delivery tracking. It enables effective management of sales and customer relationships.
6. **Customer Relationship Management (CRM) Module:**
    - The CRM module is dedicated to managing customer information, interactions, and relationships. It helps sales and marketing teams track leads, manage customer data, and improve customer service.
7. **Project Management Module:**
    - This module assists in project planning, resource allocation, task management, time tracking, cost

control, and project reporting. It is beneficial for organizations that undertake projects with specific timelines and budgets.

8. **Asset Management Module:**
    - The asset management module handles the tracking, maintenance, and utilization of physical assets within the organization. It helps optimize asset performance and reduce downtime.
9. **Warehouse Management Module:**
    - This module focuses on warehouse operations, including inventory control, stock movements, order fulfillment, and picking and packing processes.
10. **Quality Management Module:**

- The quality management module facilitates quality control and assurance processes, including inspections, non-conformance handling, corrective actions, and quality metrics tracking.

1. **Business Intelligence and Reporting Module:**

- This module provides tools for data analysis, reporting, and performance monitoring, enabling data-driven decision-making across the organization.

1. **Compliance and Regulatory Module:**

- This module helps organizations adhere to industry-specific regulations and compliance requirements, such as financial reporting standards or environmental regulations.

The selection of specific functional modules in an ERP system depends on the organization's size, industry, and specific business needs. Organizations may choose to implement all modules or select only those that align with their operational requirements. The integration of these modules provides a unified view of business processes, enabling organizations to streamline operations, improve efficiency, and make informed decisions based on real-time data.

5.7 Integration of ERP

Integration of ERP (Enterprise Resource Planning) is a crucial aspect of successfully implementing an ERP system in an organization. Integration involves connecting the various functional modules and business processes within the ERP system, as well as integrating the ERP system with other existing software applications and systems used by the organization. The goal of integration is to ensure smooth data flow, eliminate data silos, and provide a unified view of information across the organization.

There are two primary types of integration involved in ERP implementation:

1. **Internal Integration:** Internal integration refers to connecting the various functional modules within the ERP system itself. In an ERP system, different modules, such as finance, HR, inventory, and sales, are designed to work together seamlessly, sharing data and information. For example, when a sales order is entered, the ERP system should automatically update the inventory levels and financial records.
2. **External Integration:** External integration involves connecting the ERP system with other external applications and systems used by the organization, such as CRM (Customer Relationship Management), SCM (Supply Chain Management), e-commerce platforms, and business intelligence tools. External integration ensures that data flows

smoothly between the ERP system and these external systems, avoiding data duplication and discrepancies.

The process of ERP integration includes the following steps:

1. **Data Mapping:** Identifying the data fields and structures in each application that need to be integrated and mapping them to ensure they align with each other.
2. **Data Transformation:** Converting and formatting data to match the requirements of the target system during data exchange.
3. **Data Synchronization:** Establishing mechanisms to keep data synchronized and up-to-date between the ERP system and other applications in real-time or at scheduled intervals.
4. **APIs and Middleware:** Using application programming interfaces (APIs) and middleware to facilitate communication and data exchange between different systems.
5. **Testing and Validation:** Conducting thorough testing and validation to ensure that data is accurately exchanged and processed between the integrated systems.
6. **Security and Access Control:** Implementing robust security measures to protect data during integration and controlling access to sensitive information.

Benefits of ERP Integration:

1. **Streamlined Operations:** Integration ensures that data is consistently and accurately shared across all functions, reducing manual data entry and streamlining business processes.
2. **Real-time Visibility:** Integration provides real-time access to

data, allowing employees to make informed decisions based on up-to-date information.

3. **Improved Efficiency:** Automated data exchange between systems saves time and reduces errors, leading to improved efficiency in business operations.
4. **Enhanced Data Accuracy:** Integration reduces the risk of data discrepancies and duplicate entries, leading to improved data accuracy and reliability.
5. **Holistic Reporting:** Integrated data allows for comprehensive and holistic reporting, enabling better insights into overall business performance.
6. **Increased Collaboration:** Integration promotes better collaboration between different teams and departments, fostering a unified approach to achieving business objectives.
7. **Scalability:** Integrated systems are more scalable and adaptable to changes in business needs and growth.

OVERALL, ERP INTEGRATION is a critical factor in maximizing the benefits of an ERP system, enabling organizations to achieve better control, efficiency, and competitiveness in today's fast-paced business environment.

5.8 Supply chain and Customer Relationship Applications

Supply chain and customer relationship applications are essential components of an ERP (Enterprise Resource Planning) system, designed to manage and optimize key aspects of supply chain operations and customer interactions. These applications play a crucial role in streamlining processes, enhancing collaboration, and improving customer service, leading to overall efficiency and customer satisfaction.

Supply Chain Management (SCM) Application:

1. The SCM application within an ERP system focuses on managing the end-to-end supply chain operations, from procurement to order fulfillment. Key features of SCM applications include:
    - **Inventory Management:** Tracking and optimizing inventory levels, ensuring sufficient stock while minimizing carrying costs.
    - **Procurement:** Managing supplier information, purchase orders, and supplier performance to ensure timely and cost-effective sourcing.
    - **Order Management:** Processing customer orders, tracking order status, and managing order fulfillment and delivery.
    - **Demand Forecasting:** Utilizing historical data and analytics to predict future demand and plan production and inventory levels accordingly.
    - **Logistics and Distribution:** Managing transportation, warehousing, and distribution activities to ensure timely delivery of goods to customers.
    - **Supplier Collaboration:** Facilitating collaboration with suppliers to improve visibility, efficiency, and responsiveness in the supply chain.

Customer Relationship Management (CRM) Application:

1. The CRM application focuses on managing customer

interactions, sales processes, and marketing efforts. Key features of CRM applications include:

- **Contact and Account Management:** Maintaining a centralized database of customer information and interactions.
- **Sales Automation:** Managing sales leads, opportunities, and quotes to streamline the sales process.
- **Marketing Automation:** Planning, executing, and tracking marketing campaigns to generate leads and nurture customer relationships.
- **Customer Service and Support:** Managing customer inquiries, complaints, and support requests to enhance customer satisfaction.
- **Sales Analytics:** Providing insights into sales performance, customer behavior, and market trends to support data-driven decision-making.
- **Customer Engagement:** Enhancing customer engagement through personalized communication and tailored offers.

INTEGRATION BETWEEN SCM and CRM applications in an ERP system is essential for ensuring smooth flow of information and seamless coordination between supply chain operations and customer interactions. For example:

- When a customer places an order, the SCM application can automatically check inventory levels and production schedules to confirm if the order can be fulfilled on time.
- If there is a delay in order fulfillment due to inventory shortages, the CRM application can proactively notify the customer and provide an estimated delivery date.

- Customer service representatives can access real-time data on order status and shipment tracking from the SCM application to provide accurate updates to customers.

The integration of supply chain and customer relationship applications enables organizations to align their operations with customer demands, improve supply chain efficiency, and deliver exceptional customer experiences, fostering long-term customer loyalty and business growth.

Don't miss out!

Visit the website below and you can sign up to receive emails whenever SANJIVAN SAINI publishes a new book. There's no charge and no obligation.

https://books2read.com/r/B-A-NIYZ-AIFQC

BOOKS 2 READ

Connecting independent readers to independent writers.

Did you love *Management Information systems - MIS*? Then you should read *Exploring the Fundamentals of Database Management Systems*[1] by SANJIVAN SAINI!

[2]

In today's digital age, the efficient management of data is crucial for organizations of all sizes. To delve into this essential subject, we present a comprehensive overview of the book titled "Fundamentals of Database Management Systems" authored by Sanjivan Saini. This article will not only introduce you to the book but also cover key chapters and concepts, including the Introduction of DBMS, DATA MODELLING, The Relational Data Model, Codd's Rule of DBMS, SQL-99, and Introduction to SQL Programming Techniques. Let's embark on this journey to uncover the core principles of database management.

---

1. https://books2read.com/u/3nB6l5
2. https://books2read.com/u/3nB6l5

Introduction of DBMS: Building the Foundation

The book starts with a strong foundation by explaining the Introduction of Database Management Systems (DBMS). In this chapter, readers are introduced to the fundamental concepts of DBMS, the reasons why it is essential, and its role in the digital world. With a clear and concise explanation, this chapter provides a solid understanding of the subject.

DATA MODELLING: The Art of Structuring Data

Data modeling is a critical aspect of database management. The chapter on DATA MODELLING delves into the art of structuring data. It explores various data modeling techniques, their importance, and how they play a vital role in designing efficient database systems. By the end of this chapter, readers will have a profound understanding of how to model data effectively.

Codd's Rule of DBMS: Ensuring Data Integrity

Data integrity is a paramount concern in database management. Codd's Rule of DBMS is a set of guidelines developed by Dr. E.F. Codd to ensure data accuracy and consistency. This chapter explores these rules in detail, shedding light on how they are applied in real-world scenarios to maintain the quality of data within a database.

SQL-99: The Language of Databases

Structured Query Language (SQL) is the universal language of databases, and the book discusses its SQL-99 standard in a dedicated chapter. Readers will learn about the syntax, commands, and capabilities of SQL, making them proficient in querying and managing databases. This chapter serves as a valuable resource for those looking to master SQL.

Introduction to SQL Programming Techniques: Unlocking Database Potential

In the final chapter, "Introduction to SQL Programming Techniques," the book dives into advanced SQL programming methods. This section equips readers with the knowledge and skills required to harness the full potential of a database. By the end of this chapter, you'll be ready to create powerful and efficient database applications.

In conclusion, "**Fundamentals of Database Management Systems**" is a valuable resource for those who wish to understand the core concepts and principles of DBMS. With its informative chapters and in-depth explanations, it's a book that can truly elevate your knowledge in the field of database management. So, dive into this insightful read and unlock the power of managing data effectively.

Also by SANJIVAN SAINI

Business strategy books

Procedure and Documentation in Supply Chain Management
Exploring the Fundamentals of Database Management Systems
Cold chain Business Planning and Strategy: Design, Retrofit And Maintenance Of Cold Storages And Pack Houses
Management Information systems - MIS

Standalone

Logistics in Manufacturing, Supply Chain, and Distribution
E-commerce
Engineering Economics & Accountancy :Managerial Economics
The Essence of Innovation
Introduction to Reverse Logistics
Material Handling Repair and Maintenance of Equipment
Port Terminals System - Conveyor and Equipment Maintenance
"Packaging
����� ��������-3: ����� �� ��� ����� ���
����, ������ �� ���� ������
Fundamentals of Logistics and Warehousing